Praise for Dana Ross

Thru Thick & Thin *is an incredible story of real love through the eyes of a loved one. We live in a cruel world where we are constantly being judged. Obesity remains the #1 killer in this country and as a man who was a biscuit over 400 pounds, I never stopped to think about the weight my excess weight put on my wife and family.* Thru Thick & Thin *is a wonderful blueprint for others to lovingly and yet respectfully address this dreaded disease.*

-Jamie Dukes
CEO/Founder
Put Up Your Dukes Foundation
"Keep'n It Real Love"

"If you want to light up your life and health in amazing ways, get to know this amazing couple and their journey through the captivating words of Dana Rosser. Anyone who gets to know them and read their story will always feel blessed and thankful for the gift of health and happiness they bring. Their smiles and great personalities alone will draw you in, but their written words of how to overcome the many misunderstandings of weight gain, food, diet, and health with information that is at the sometime scientific and spiritual is a must for every American as we face the most serious risk to our lives and the lives of millions of people.

The risks from obesity in our country today affect the majority of our population. It threatens every one of us every day—way more than terrorists, auto accidents, gun shots, yet gets so much less attention. In most cases, the answers are understanding food choices, but there are so many other factors that diets, a salad, a pill, or a slap on the back can't address.

Dana and Butch's journey enlightens and educates us all and will help you live a longer happier life."

-Paul Alan Wetter, M.D. F.A.C.O.G, F.A.C.S.
Professor, Emeritus University of Miami School of Medicine
Chairman Society of Laparoendoscopic Surgeons

---

that is not directly or indirectly impacted. Those affected can hope to begin a successful journey to address this issue. This book is a must read."

-Rod Paige, Ph.D.
Former U.S. Secretary of Education
(January 20, 2001-January 20, 2005)

"Dana Mitchell Rosser's book, Thru Thick & Thin, *has finally released the elephant in the room. Thru Thick & Thin takes you to the core of what many keep inside. Her book has given a penetrating voice unlike no other. It has also given you tools and a way to approach this very sensitive matter. It brings about a conversation, that a person living with someone they love dearly, and suffers with obesity, feels on a daily bases.*

Obesity is one of the most sensitive conversations for Americans to have. At the end of the day, I hope and pray that Thru Thick & Thin *will touch, save lives, and bring awareness to all parties involved who find themselves in this type of relationship. It is time to share what you have kept hidden in your closet before it kills you.*

Thank you, Dana, for opening your life and heart for those of us that need to know that Thru Thick & Thin, *it will be okay."*

-Lauren F.

"I am so proud of Dana and Butch. Their story is more than a self-help strategy; it's even more than a raw honest look at obesity; and it's much more than an inspirational novel. It's a love story, uncensored and real. The kind of story that changes you somewhere deep inside, and the change is for the better."

-Terrence M. Fullum, M.D. FACS
Professor of Surgery
Howard University College of Medicine
Chief, Division of General Surgery
Chief, Division of Minimally Invasive and Bariatric Surgery
Medical Director, Center for Wellness and Weight Loss Surgery

Thru Thick & Thin

Facing Obesity thru the Eyes of a Loved One

Dana M. Rosser

To my God and to my family and to my purpose.
Thank you.

"You may be the only mirror through which
people are able to see themselves."
-Ella Gooden

TABLE OF CONTENTS

FOREWORD

I n her new book, *Thru Thick & Thin,* Dana Rosser, author and wife of a prominent surgeon (Dr. James "Butch" Rosser Jr.), who was challenged by severe obesity, uniquely sheds light on the emotional hardships and challenges faced by family members of severely obese people.

As Dr. Rosser's surgeon (and friend), I can attest to the myriad health and self-esteem challenges he and millions of other people (20 million Americans with severe obesity!) have faced with their struggle against the "O" word, *obesity.* Doctors with immense medical knowledge and enviable professional success are supposed to be immune to obesity. However, as Dana points out in her book, while many people have prejudice against obese people, obesity itself is an equal opportunity disease effecting people of all race and socioeconomic status, even famous doctors!

Recognizing that the root of all prejudice is ignorance, Dana Rosser attempts and greatly succeeds to educate us through her compelling story, about the unfounded stereotypes and shame that "nutritionally challenged" people face every day. She shows how the critical support role of spouses and family members can offset such challenges and enable their loved one to seek and obtain greatly needed treatment—in this case, bariatric surgery.

Thru Thick & Thin is a story of triumph over severe obesity and the arduous journey of both patient and family members. Anyone who struggles with obesity or cares deeply for a loved one with obesity should read this book!

-Philip Schauer, M.D.
Professor of Surgery
Cleveland Clinic Lerner College of Medicine
Cleveland, Ohio

Preface

GOD, I AM SO TIRED!

Yes, I am tired—not physically tired so much as mentally exhausted. God, I know you want me to write something, but I don't know exactly what you want me to say. I feel so drained from talking about obesity and how it affected me. For me, it's old news.

Yes, in my soul I know the story is everyday news for so many people. I know millions of people are waiting for me to finish this book. I want them to know that I understand their pain, but I can't get to them to tell them. Every time I think about this book, I become tired and fearful. I am sick of myself and my lack of desire to complete it. Do I have a million and one things to do beside write this book? Of course, but God, you won't let me forget it. Why? Why me?

I can't get past the audacity to think that I could write something to help others. All my life, I have had a heart for people. As far back as I can remember, I have always wanted to uplift others; I love being their cheerleader. Encouragement has always come so naturally for me. I love to see people laugh. I guess maybe that is why you chose me, God.

Maybe you wanted me to help others laugh again.
Just maybe you want me to help them realize there is no guilt in feeling
what they feel.
God, help me reach my true potential in doing your will.

-Dana Rosser
Florida, 2015

Introduction

Tell Your Story...Set Someone Free!

Someone once said to me, "Dana, you are a lighthouse for the world. Tell your story; let your light shine and set someone free."

So, many years later, I am doing just that—sharing my story of living and loving someone who suffers with obesity. Being apprehensive about telling my journey is an understatement to say the least. First, I didn't want to feel judged by those who may misunderstand my intent or question my genuine heart-felt concern for spouses, family, friends, loved ones, and supporters who delicately walk this walk every day.

Secondly, I must admit I was afraid in some small way I knew in my heart that this book would be a success. Not so much based on the fact that my writing is Pulitzer Prize winning material, but because I know anyone who reads my story can relate or has been in contact with someone who suffers with obesity.

Obesity has reached epidemic proportions globally; more than one third (34.9% or 78.6 million) of US adults are obese. Obesity-related conditions include heart disease, stroke, Type 2 Diabetes, and certain types of cancer are some of the leading causes of preventable death. Apart from tobacco, there is perhaps no greater harm to the collective health in the US than obesity.

Worldwide, too, obesity's health effects are deep and vast—and they have a real and lasting impact on communities, on nations, and most importantly, on individuals, today and across future generations. In the US, among adults under the age of seventy, obesity is second only to tobacco in the number of deaths it causes each year. As tobacco use continues to decline, and obesity rates continue to rise, the number of deaths due to obesity may soon exceed that of tobacco.

Obesity is a major contributor to the global burden of chronic disease and disability. It is a complex condition, with serious social and psychological dimensions, affecting virtually all ages and socioeconomic groups. The estimated annual medical cost of the obesity in the US was $147 billion in 2008; the medical cost for the people who are obese were $1429 higher than those of normal weight. We have to get a handle on this disease, especially for our future generations.[1]

Whether it is your family member, co-worker, friend, member of your church, or a stranger you meet, you are certain to interact with someone who has this obesity challenge. Through reading this book, you can respond with care and love, and act upon what is relevant for you. You can also share this book with those who need it.

Possibly being labeled an expert without all the degrees or certifications behind my name frightened me, but I could not let that minor fact deter me from my truth. I've lived my truth for over twenty years.

My reality is I lived with a morbidly obese person, and my experience both educated and credentialed me.

Mine is the story of a young woman who fell madly in love with a 460-pound. southern gentleman, Dr. James "Butch" Rosser, whom she subsequently marries and enters the world of obesity up close and personal. The cruel reality of discrimination against the obese, the feelings of helplessness, the diminished quality of life, and the fear of losing him stifled and hindered my life daily. Yet, the love I had for my husband never wavered; I was in this relationship for life. Where could I go to seek help without feeling like I betrayed my husband? I was truly the only real friend he had who accepted him unconditionally. Yet, I needed help to deal with my thoughts, emotions, and responses. Whom could I trust with my true feelings? Why weren't there any resources at the book stores or online that could help me put my feelings in order?

I felt I couldn't tell him how I truly felt; it would crush him. He already felt so insecure and self-conscious because of his weight. So, where could I go? Who could I turn to? I was reminded of Toni Morrison's quip, "If there's a book that you want to read, but it hasn't been written yet, then you must write it." That is why I wrote this book. There were limited resources available and I knew I had to be the change I wanted to see. So, I wrote a book that:

- Validates your real, heartfelt, conflicted feelings.
- Gives tips on coping with a loved one's obesity.
- Tells the stories of others who have gone through this same challenge and either came out triumphantly on the other side or failed trying their best and making healthy decisions for themselves and their obese loved one.
- Teaches about the causes of obesity in lay terms without the medical or academic or even nutritional jargon, clichés, or obscure Latin nomenclature.
- Is informative not only to the supporter, but to the person who suffers with this disease.

In understanding how complex obesity is and its effects on the entire family, an author like myself never knows if sharing one vital piece of the puzzle in a book could be the key, motivating factor that will spark an "aha" moment for the reader's loved one. Our hope is it will give readers the hope and drive they need to get healthy, not just for themselves, but for everyone affected by obesity and the issues surrounding it.

This book is **not** a "fat" bashing book. So, if this is what you are looking for, please return it immediately and get your money back. This is a true story built on a foundation of love. You have to be willing to dig deep and come from a good place to benefit from my journey. Learn from my story and insights!

---

*When I say things that resonate with you, use what I have learned to grow, be equipped, and help others—that is your duty as a human being—**pay it forward.***

IMPORTANT: I encourage you to read this book completely through to the end. You will notice at the end of each chapter, there are questions and actions you may want to take. Hold off on asking those questions or taking those actions until you have completed reading the book all the way through at least once. I can imagine at some places you may feel overwhelmed by emotions. Let yourself cry, laugh, feel deeply, experience grief or sadness, or any emotions my book may evoke in you.

After you have read this book completely through once, you will come to my Final Word of Encouragement with instructions on your options for what do to next. Don't rush. Allow this book to soak into your mind and your heart.

I pray you find value in this book and you are enlightened in some small way on this journey called "life." Read with an open heart and mind, and be ready to receive a miracle of insight, education, wisdom, knowledge, understanding, and practical application. God bless you on your journey.

ACKNOWLEDGMENTS

Special thanks to my husband (Dr. James "Butch" Rosser Jr.) for your undying support throughout this book and giving me the privilege to love you *Thru Thick and Thin*. To my children (Kevin, Duane, Nikki, Taylor, and Tianna) for your encouragement and authentic contributions to this project. I love you all. To the best sister, Dawn Mitchell, a girl could ask for – thank you for being my number one cheerleader. To my parents (Yvonne Mitchell and Mercer Mitchell Sr.), my brother Mercer Mitchell Jr., and the rest of my extended family and close friends for your prayers and well wishes for this book throughout the years...I love you all to the moon and back.

I would also like to thank Bishop Joey Johnson, Pastor Cathy Johnson, Rebecca Hodge, Lauren F., and Sarah H., for your prayers, comments, and contributions to this book. I truly could not have finished it without you.

Thank you to Xulon Press for publishing this book and a special thanks to Dr. Larry Keefauver for being the best editor and writing coach...you rock! Thank you to Nissa Grayson for an awesome cover design and Stacy Pierce Photography for the beautiful headshot.

I would like to express my gratitude to the many people who saw me through this book and to all those who provided support, talked things over, read, wrote, offered comments, allowed me to quote their remarks, endorsed the book, and assisted in any other way...thank you, thank you, thank you.

Last but certainly not least, a big thank you to my God. You would not let me give up on this book. Thank you for loving me, pushing me, opening doors, and giving me the courage to help others. To God be the glory!

-1-

MIRROR...MIRROR

There are support groups and diet centers all over the country to help the nutritionally challenged address their issues. Yet, one group of individuals who are key to an obese person's recovery often go unrecognized: *the loved ones of the person battling obesity.* Spouses, family members, and friends of the nutritionally challenged live in a unique, challenging, and often secretive world that no one wants to address.

As a loved one relating to someone who is obese, there are so many emotions that we experience, but keep secret because we are afraid or ashamed to admit our feelings for fear of hurting the one we love. Whether the issue is concern for their health, intimacy, quality of life, self-esteem, or any other life situation, loved ones often tread through the issues softly and quietly.

Today, most everyone knows someone who is suffering from obesity, so there will likely come a time when these issues will need to be addressed. I hope sharing my story will help others to explore the world of obesity through the eyes of a loved one. Sharing can be a step toward helping our society realize the obesity epidemic affects many more people than the 34.9 percent of the population (US adults) who actually are obese. It also deeply affects the family, friends, and loved ones of the obese individual.

In researching this subject, I often wondered when some individuals spoke about their loved one's challenge with weight if they came from a good place or tried to be a "closet" fat hater. Did they have real concerns, were they seeking solutions or were they just looking for another reason to beat them down? More often than not, the people I have interviewed have had a genuine concern for their loved ones and wanted to be heard and not misunderstood or judged.

What about you? Why do you want more information on this subject?

What are your true feelings about having a loved one who is obese? Not wanting to come forward to divulge your true feelings is a "big" problem that we as supporters face. Telling the "real" truth was the enemy in my world for a long time. I felt if I expressed my feelings about this delicate subject, people wouldn't look at me the same. They would think my marriage was all a lie and I never loved him like I said I did. I would probably be the one to get "beat down." I already beat myself up because of my feelings of guilt and shame. I truly didn't need others adding even more of a whipping to my already bruised spirit.

So, I said all that to say I am the "real deal." I know this is not the easiest subject to open up about, but it is clear this discussion is long overdue and the time is now for it to be uncovered and dealt with, once and for all.

It is imperative for you, my readers, to get to know me as a person and to know my heart and my intentions for writing this special book to help and encourage you.

I want you to know the struggles I have faced in my own life. Though it was not obesity, I had a struggle with my own physical appearance and being wrongly judged and ridiculed for being "me." I'm referring to my struggles before I met Butch. I was tall and skinny with a lot of complexes. I truly believe God allowed me to go through certain trials and tribulations so I could be prepared to show compassion and empathy for the journey He knew I would have to walk one day. My heart is right where it is supposed to be: ready to be clear in my truth, clear in my intent, and clear in my desire to set someone free. That being said, "Let's get to know Dana."

My Personal History

Dana Marie Mitchell was born in Akron, Ohio, to Mercer and Yvonne Mitchell. By the way, Akron, Ohio, is the home of Lebron James (Cleveland Cavalier star basketball player). We are all so proud of him. Okay, back to me. I grew up in a lower middle class home on the west side of Akron. As a youngster, I was a little shy at times because I was quite tall and thin. I didn't know how good I had it back then, especially the thin part. I was the middle child of three and the tallest. Currently, I stand 6'2," but I remember when I was 5'9" in the sixth grade—that was the worst! I always felt a little awkward and out of sorts. Teased uncontrollably at school, I was always the brunt of jokes and sarcastic remarks like, "How's the weather up there, Dana?" and, "Hey, Olive Oil, where is Popeye?" I was called "Skinny Minnie," "Tree Trunk," "Boney Maroney," and worst of all, "Cheryl Twigs" instead of Cheryl Tiegs (She was a famous, skinny model back in the day). There were so many other names that thankfully I have erased from my mental rolodex.

I learned what others thought or said about me didn't define who I was.

People always seem to have the need to tell me that I am "tall," like that is a revelation to me. I have always wanted to say back to them, ***"I know, you idiot!"*** Now, I know most people didn't mean anything by it, but when you hear it over and over and over again, you start to get a complex. "Okay, I'm different I get it." I could never wear all the cute styles that the other kids wore because everything was always too short on me or too big in the waist. My Nana, bless her heart, had to make some of my clothes.

Nana could sew, but the simplicity patterns she picked for me did not quite keep up with the fashion trend of the 70s, if you know what I mean. I know she did her best, and I was always so grateful I did not have to wear highwaters (pants that are unintentionally short in the hem), but the "cuteness factor" was lost. I would always see all the latest styles at K-Mart. Unfortunately, I knew in my heart they would not fit me.

Oh, and don't get me started on my feet! My feet were another major issue. I wore a size ten shoe when there were no cute size ten shoes on the planet. I remember one night my prayer to God was to shrink my feet from a size ten to a size seven by the time I woke up the next morning. I remember really wanting to get these cute baby doll shoes that all my friends had, but unfortunately the shoes did not come in a size ten. To my dismay as I awoke in the morning, I looked down at my feet and guess what? Nothing happened! I was so mad at God because He knew I wanted those shoes. I wondered why He couldn't grant me this one wish. I guess I thought God was some magic genie character. I remember having to wear this one black pair of shoes to school that even my loving Nana would have never worn, but my dad made me wear them anyway.

Back then, my parents had to go to a specialty store in Cleveland for shoes which were expensive, but the style factor was totally lost. Looking back on it now, my parents did their best to provide for me and wanted their tall baby to have quality shoes. The next time I was made to wear those ugly shoes, I snuck another pair in my backpack and switched them out when I got to school.

Mitchell Family

Life with My Older Brother

Unfortunately, my older brother, Mercer, Jr., who was at school, saw I switched the shoes, and went home and told my parents. My big brother was a great basketball player who played point guard, but I knew he secretly envied my height. He would have killed to have been 6'2". As fate would have it, I had no desire to play basketball or any sports for that fact. Mercer was all of 5'8" in high school, and by sixth grade, I was already 5'9". We are two years apart, so you know he was upset, to say the least. I still crack up thinking about how he would have me in the backyard trying to show me how to play basketball. I had no clue nor did I want to find a clue on how to play.

One day, Mercer got so frustrated at me because I did not know how to guard him. Trying to guard him, I tripped and fell so hard, I scraped my knee so the "white meat" showed. Ouch! To this day I have a scar on my left knee that I call the "Potty" scar. "Potty" is his nickname. (Don't ask about how he got that nickname, *please!*) To this day, Potty stands up on his tippy toes to try to be as tall as me when we take pictures. He is so cute, though, and has since accepted I will always be taller than him even though he is older than me. I love him so!

Trying to Blend In

Since I was always so much taller than everyone else, I had a tendency to slouch trying to blend in. My mother would always say, "Dana, stand up straight girl, be proud of your height." How could I? I was always taller than my teachers in elementary school and extremely taller than the other kids, especially the boys heading into junior high. When we would take our class pictures, I would always have to stand in the back with the teachers. On one hand, I felt like I was someone important standing with the teachers, but on the other hand, I felt so detached from my classmates. I was constantly reminded I was different.

> *Early in life, a child may think being different is a liability. I've learned being different is an asset—I am unique and talented in ways that give me an edge in life.*

Even my little sister, Dawn, was "normal height." No other girls in the Mitchell family had the kind of height I had. "Why me?" I would ask.

I needed some self-confidence, so my mother enrolled me in a "Wendy Ward" program at the Montgomery Ward Department Store on the east side of Akron. Wendy Ward was a program geared toward enhancing confidence in young ladies through teaching etiquette, poise, and introducing them to modeling. Believe me, I was no "model." I may have had the height to model, but that was it. I do remember at the end of the course, there was a graduation ceremony in the form of a fashion show in which all the young ladies had to participate. Lord, I was so scared. I thought, *You mean to tell me I have to model on a runway, which meant I would have to walk in front of family, friends, and strangers without falling on my face? What in the world?*

Our instructors informed us that our outfits were to be chosen from the department store, which at the time I thought was so cool. We literally had free rein of the store and could pick out whatever we wanted. Well, the Wendy Ward graduation day finally arrived, and to my surprise, I was told I did well. Not truly buying into the idea that I could be the next Cheryl Twiggs, I mean "Cheryl Tiegs," I tempered my enthusiasm a bit. After that fashion show, I was approached about modeling in many fashion shows throughout the Akron area. It felt like I finally found something that my height and weight would serve to be an asset for me instead of a liability. Thinking back, I was always told I was pretty when I was growing up, but for some reason, in my head, those compliments never registered.

Often the reality of who we are
is determined by our inner perceptions,
not our outward realities.

After Wendy Ward, I decided to get serious about modeling. My mother enrolled me in a modeling school in the area and I began to pick up little modeling jobs here and there as I continued to go to school. I became well known in the community because I would model at the local malls, and would be chosen to model for salons at their annual hair shows, church fashion shows, or any other events that needed models. People would stop me and say, "I saw you at so and so's fashion show, you are really good." In some ways, modeling provided an escape for me from the inner negative thoughts and feelings I had formed about myself. When I would model on stage, I totally became someone else; I kind of had an alter ego. I had this positive "attitude" on stage that exuded confidence. I put on this performance mask for everyone, because modeling is what everyone seemed to think I should do—that or play basketball.

Don't get me wrong. I did not hate modeling, but in some ways modeling felt phony to me. I often felt like a piece of meat when I modeled. The people back stage would make me up so beautifully, and give me all these magnificent clothes and jewelry, furs, etc., and then push me out there to perform without even a, "How are you today, Dana?" They were focused on my external appearance. I often thought, *These people don't know the real Dana and they don't want to get to know me. Just get out there and perform.* I do know for sure the folks I worked with cared about me, but it was my own internal struggle that made me question my worth.

So many times after the show, people would be waiting to congratulate me and give me all kinds of praise, which I appreciated. Then they would notice the person on the stage was not the person that I am. It often appeared to disappoint them in a way. After the show, I was quite shy and not as flamboyant as my stage act. Even though I had found something I was presumably good at, I still didn't feel quite content with modeling. I thought I only had two options in life because of my appearance—modeling or basketball. After all, aren't those the only two things a girl my size could do? I let society dictate what I could or could not do. I guess, in my eyes, my height was being exploited.

Exploited? Yes, I felt that my destiny was determined by others and that was a form of exploitation to me. Of course, those were not the only two options that I had, but society would not let me be a beautiful, funny, Christian young lady who happened to be tall without any expectations. I had to do something with this height, so maybe that is why I wasn't totally in love with modeling.

> *One's height, weight, appearance, or size doesn't determine one's vocation or destiny. It doesn't define one's personality or worth. Have you ever felt like your physical attributes are an asset or liability to you?*

My high school years brought many different challenges. The boys finally caught up with my height. Thank God. I started to fill out up top only, so I wasn't as skinny. Hallelujah. I was still into modeling, but now a new issue arose. Some people thought I thought I was cute. What? You must be kidding. Because I was presumably pretty, tall, had pretty hair, and modeled, I had to be stuck up. What else could I be? How about nice, sweet, and fun-loving; did that ever cross anyone's mind? Let me answer that for you. No! So, now I was judged because of looks again. When would it end? I wished people would have gotten to know me before they assumed all this stuff.

Once I established myself with my classmates, they finally started to come around and see the real, goofy, silly Dana. Even the guys judged me in some ways. I was never asked to Homecoming my junior year because the guys assumed I already had a date. How did they assume that? Well, they said, "We knew as pretty as you are, you had guys lined up to ask you out." Wrong, wrong, wrong. Here I was on the homecoming court and dateless. I had to ask Kendrick Woods at the last minute to take me to Homecoming. Thank God, he agreed. Thanks Kendrick! I was voted best looking and best personality in my senior year. How ironic to me. The judgment of my physical appearance had come full circle.

Modeling for *Ebony*?

By college, I believe I finally came into my own. I did not quite know what my career path would be, maybe psychology, social work, business, or even modeling. At the time, *Ebony* magazine was auditioning models for their annual Fashion Fair Show. My mother told me that I should send in my pictures. I didn't want to because I felt like I did not have a chance. I can't remember if my mom sent the pictures in or if I did, but either way they called me to come audition. Mind you, at that time they only picked fifty girls out of the whole country to fly in to Chicago to audition. I was floored they asked me.

At the time, I was 6'2" and weighed 138 pounds. I remember the *Ebony* staff told me that I needed to lose weight before I came to the audition. I felt like I was already a walking bone with boobs, but I would try to lose the weight. I went on the grapefruit diet, some beet and boiled egg diet, and did not find one I could stick to. I can't quite remember how much they told me to lose, but I believe it might have been between five and ten pounds. I tried my best to lose the ten pounds, but I knew I had fallen short. I had never in my life had to be on a diet, so I didn't take it too seriously. I was always told I was too skinny. I guess in a way I hoped once they saw me, they wouldn't notice or mind me being a pound or two off their ideal weight of 128 pounds.

As I boarded the plane at the small Akron-Canton Airport, I thought to myself, *Here you go Dana, you may become the next Beverly Johnson. Maybe this is the start of something big and maybe, just maybe, you'll get to travel the world and become famous as America's next top model.*

As I entered that audition hall, I was surrounded by so many beautiful women. This one model in particular stood out to me. She was as tall as I was, slender, and she had dark brown flawless skin with the most beautiful blue eyes you would ever want to see. She looked like she was from some exotic island. Wow! I thought, *What in the world am I, Dana Marie Mitchell, from little old Akron, Ohio doing here?* I had to do some serious soul searching. I would say to myself, "Okay, Dana, you are not chopped liver now; you were chosen just like these other women; you were one of fifty, too, don't get it twisted girl!"

I thought, *Dana this is it, put your game face/alter ego on, and get out there and strut your stuff!* I remember my hometown was so proud of me. It was in the local paper that I auditioned for the Ebony Fashion Fair, so I did not want to let them down or my family, for that matter. My mother drove from Akron to Chicago to be there for me. Through all of this, I know my mom was proud of me. She was always my biggest fan at all the many fashion shows and pageants that I participated in. A lot of times she would enter me in pageants and contests and Lord knows I did not want to do it.

Dana's modeling day; Dana at a pageant

Looking back now, those activities contributed to who I am today and the resilience that I learned from each experience.

At the audition, the staff weighed us before we went on the runway and I weighed 135 pounds. Thank God that today the modeling industry has finally changed its weight restrictions for models because truly, that is thin for someone who is 6'2." As I walked on to that runway, I thought how far I had come from Wendy Ward School to auditioning for one of the most prestigious fashion shows in the country. Strutting my stuff on stage had become an old habit for me, so I wasn't that nervous. As I focused my eyes on the judges, I studied their every move. One of the judges seemed to be interested in me. I saw them jotting notes down and huddling together. Then the words that would change my life forever came out of one of the judge's mouths, *she is too fat.*

They Called Me *"Fat!"*

Wait a minute, back up, maybe I read her lips wrong. Did she just say what I think she said? By no means am I a professional lip reader, but it is not hard to read the word, "fat" out of someone's lips. I was glad she did not say it out loud over the microphone for the whole world to hear. It was like everything in the room slowed down and my heart sank. The word, *"fat."*

*What? **Fat!** That word is a universal downer. If you ever want to instantly make someone feel bad, tell them that they are fat.*

As they said, "Thank you," and yelled, "Next!" for the girl waiting behind me, I went into an abyss of some sort. It was like I wanted to cry, but I was relieved, mad, and also proud. I wanted to eat, but I thought I was too fat. Yet, most of all, I walked away with clarity. At that moment, I knew I did not want to have a job where I would be judged solely on my looks. Looks can come and go. In the modeling industry, so can your job. As they read the names of the young ladies who had made the final cut, I knew my name would not be on that list.

Of course, I was disappointed, but looking back, I realized God had ordered my steps so I would do the will He had for me. I think the hardest part of that experience had to be telling my mom I didn't make it. Even though I knew she would love me no matter what, I felt bad that she had driven the six-plus hours to hear they had not picked me because of my weight. Anything else, but that! I may never know if my weight was the only reason I was not picked, but it doesn't matter now. I believe knowing that one reason would come to be a defining moment in my life and shape the way I felt about myself and others, *forever*.

Society as we know it has always put a high premium on physical attractiveness. Most of the time we see at images in a magazines or television that simply are not even real. These models or actors have been digitally enhanced, touched up, made up twice over, and everything else. We as consumers try to attain a look that they don't even have naturally. Isn't that crazy? We are trying to look like someone who doesn't even exist. Now that is sick!

Perfection of any type is unattainable, because we are all imperfect human beings, and that is okay! Someone needs to start a campaign with the motto:

"It's okay; I'm not perfect and neither are you."

How freeing that would be to our children. How much more creative our society would be if people could be who they were meant to be without the pressure of having to be perfect or look perfect. However, strides are being made to bring "real" people back into the media. Dove's campaign of "Real Beauty" comes to mind, and more full-figure actresses are becoming more visible in Hollywood. We are seeing more "full-figured models" featured in magazines and that is a great step in the right direction. I still don't understand why they call them "full-figure" models. They should be called "healthy figure models." I don't know, but that word "full" makes me feel like they put these models in the category of being enormous. It gives the presumption that these models are not normal.

So, this the journey that God used to prepare my heart and demeanor to be able to become my husband's biggest cheerleader through his challenges with obesity. By no means am I saying our journeys are comparable, but I trust you can connect with me and know I understand living with labels and being judged only by one's appearance—tall, fat, skinny, and the like. I can connect with the judgment and societal responses to being different, the feelings of hopelessness, and the desire to be accepted the way I am. Even though my experiences may be different than yours, we have similar challenges and struggles. I, too, have been a victim in some ways and that has allowed me to have a vantage point of empathy for others. For that, I am truly grateful.

> *I always find beauty in things that are odd & imperfect—*
> *they are much more interesting.*
> -Marc Jacobs

Ask Yourself...

- *What are your inner thoughts and childhood memories of how you saw yourself and thought of others in terms of fat or skinny, beautiful or ugly, tall or short, etc.? Did you feel good or bad about your physical appearance?*
- *What childhood names were you called? Do you still feel pain from them?*
- *How would you evaluate your self-confidence on a scale of one (extremely low) to ten (very strong)?*
- *How did your experiences growing up and cultural or conventional wisdom shape your present attitudes about obesity, nutrition, and people who are overweight?*
- *Who is the person in your family who is obese? Are you talking with that person about their obesity and how you feel about it? If not, what feelings do you have about honest conversations about your feelings—shame, guilt, fear, rejection, pain, or what?*

- *What words would you use to describe your physical appearance? What words would you use to describe your obese family member's physical appearance?*

Would You Take These Actions?

- Think about who might be a friend you can share the content of this book with and who can be a support person for you.
- Begin keeping a journal of your thoughts, conversations, and actions as you read through this book.
- Write down a description of each person's attitude in your "growing up" family and your present family toward obesity (including your own).

-2-

"Is *She* with *Him*?"

After graduating from college with a marketing degree and landing a successful job, I thought I had a handle on most things in life. I came from a good family and had friends, and a good church with a bright future. My life was relatively good. In 1992, I met the man of my dreams, James "Butch" Rosser, M.D., a successful surgeon. I absolutely fell for him. Butch was from Mississippi and he had that "southern thang" going on, and I loved it. His smile was contagious and his heart was like no other. For the first time in my life, I felt like there was someone in the world who loved me unconditionally. Butch was *the one* for me. By the way, I need to also mention Butch stood 6'4" tall and weighed 460 pounds. Yes, he was morbidly obese. Forgetting that fact was impossible because his obesity was what everyone seemed to fixate on during our courtship.

I met Butch at The House of the Lord Church in Akron, Ohio. I had known of him through my Nana who worked at Akron General Medical Center in the surgical unit. She always spoke so highly of this bigger-than-life surgeon who was so kind and talented. Butch was a world-renowned laparoscopic (general) surgeon and well respected in the community and abroad. Ironically enough, he did a small procedure on my mother many years prior and I remembered her praising him for his bedside manner and professionalism. As you could imagine, on that particular Sunday morning when he asked to speak with me for a moment, I was taken aback. My friend, Kim

Johnson and I were laughing and chatting in the corner as usual after church. She noticed Butch was standing around like he was waiting for someone. I didn't know at the time that "someone" was me.

She said "Dana, I think Dr. Rosser is waiting for you."

Starting Our Relationship

I thought to myself, *He can't be waiting for me, can he?*

Sure enough, after I finished my conversation with Kim, Butch came up to me with that southern swag and said, "Hi, Dana. Do you mind if I talk with you for a minute?"

I said, "Sure," and we proceeded to walk to a much quieter corner.

I couldn't help but notice people watching Butch and me like a hawk in the church corridor. Butch had recently gotten a divorce and was an eligible bachelor, so I guess people were curious. I was single and had broken off a long relationship. I was not trying to get into another one anytime soon. The attention we received from others was definitely unwarranted in my eyes.

When we walked to a quiet spot, he asked me if I could help him with a problem he had. I thought to myself, *How could I possibly help this man? He is brilliant beyond belief. What in God's name am I going to say? I don't even know him. Oh my gosh!*

Uncontrolled intimidation ran through my body, but with a smile, I said, "Yes, if I can."

He then said, "Do you ever eat alone?"

I thought to myself, *Did he just say what I think he said?* Here I thought he would ask little ole me some rocket science question that God knows I would have never had the answer for, but instead he asked me if I ever eat alone. Really?

Breathing a sigh of relief because I knew the answer to this question, I said, "Yes, I do."

He then said, "Do you like eating alone?"

I had no idea where all this was leading, but I played along with it and answered him, "No, I do not like eating alone."

With a sheepish grin he uttered the words that would change our lives forever, "Well, if you don't like eating alone, and I don't like eating alone then maybe we should eat together and that would solve that problem."

I wanted to laugh so bad as I thought to myself, *If this was a pickup line, it was really cute.* I told him that I would love to enjoy a meal with him and looked forward to getting to know him better. Again, in my eyes this was a meal and nothing more.

I was at a place in my life where I needed to get to know Dana. I had been in a long-term relationship and was not interested in dating anyone or getting serious. Needless to say, we exchanged numbers and went to dinner that next Friday. We met at a restaurant called "Beaus" in the valley. Beaus was known for its great cuisine and ambiance, so I was excited when he suggested we meet there. Butch had called and told me that he was running a little late for dinner due to a surgery, but he was on his way. I immediately thought, *Wow, that was so considerate of him to think of me and my time. What a nice guy.*

When I arrived at the restaurant, the hostess asked me if I had a reservation and I said it was under Dr. Rosser's name.

She smiled and said, "Oh, we just love him," which made me know he frequented this restaurant quite a bit.

I wondered if this was the restaurant where he ate alone. She asked me where I would prefer to sit; I immediately chose a booth.

She said, "I think Dr. Rosser would be more comfortable at a table instead of a booth."

I immediately said, "Oh yes, that's fine," but I felt so awkward.

I should have known he would be more comfortable at a table; after all, Butch was a big guy. How dumb and inconsiderate of me. What was I thinking? As I sat there, beating myself up for not being sensitive to his size, I wondered what else should I be aware of. The last thing I want to do is make anyone feel awkward or self-conscious about anything. Shortly after I was seated, I saw him come through the door and my stomach started doing somersaults. I quickly wondered what that was all about. I was just having dinner, so where was that feeling coming from? It wasn't a nervous type of feeling; it was more of excitement.

> **Starting a relationship with a morbidly obese person immediately brings to mind questions about what's awkward. Do we or do we not talk about food, weight, where to sit, and what to do? Have you ever thought about such things?**

Earlier in the week, we had talked on the phone a couple of times and had gotten to know each other quite well. I have to admit, I was excited to have dinner with him. The evening couldn't have gone better. We talked and laughed like old friends. I enjoyed his company. It was refreshing to see someone of his caliber be so down-to-earth and real; he was delightful. We loved the same music, movies, food, and most of all we both loved to laugh. He asked me if I would like to go out again and I eagerly agreed. As a matter of fact, we went out several times and soon I was smitten! So much for my thinking I would have a simple meal with him.

Butch and me in Chinatown (New York)

Our Courtship and the "Touchy" Issues Surrounding "Big"

During our courtship, people would question my intentions on being with Butch. "Is she dating him because he's a surgeon? Surely she couldn't love him; he's huge!" I am not blind. I could see Butch was morbidly obese. Why other people thought I was deaf, dumb, and blind for choosing to be with him, I will never know. When I looked at him, I saw so much more than a morbidly obese person. I saw a jewel. It didn't take me long to come to find out what a lonely and cruel world it had always been for Butch in his battle with morbid obesity. I could see where people would have been intimidated with his size. At 6'4" and 460 pounds, people couldn't help but notice him as he walked into a room. I remember strangers would ask him if he was a bodyguard, professional football player, professional wrestler, preacher, or a bouncer.

Nobody could have prepared me for the "up close and personal" world of obesity that I was about to enter with Butch. Mind you, I had been exposed to family members and friends who suffered with weight issues, but not to the full extent of the day-to-day struggle that comes with morbid obesity. From day one, people made comments to me regarding how "big" Butch was.

Using the word "big" masked the real adjective that I could tell they wanted to use: "fat."

By using the more politically correct term, people tried to open the door for me to comment on Butch's weight. When put in that situation, I usually said something like, "Yes, he is a big guy and the sweetest person I know," or "Yes, he is my big teddy bear." What did they expect me to say? "Yeah, ain't he big though? He needs to lose some weight, girl. Don't you think so?"

The fact that people actually thought I would bash the person I adored was unbelievable to me. I did have genuine concerns regarding Butch's health and weight, but the backdoor approach people used in an attempt to get me to talk about it was maddening. Were they concerned for his health or were they taking the opportunity to be a "fat hater"?

I did hate it when people would bring up his weight to me because deep down inside, I knew he needed to lose weight. Perhaps secretly I didn't want to deal with it. I fell in love with him and that should be that.

I knew if he didn't take drastic measures and take control of his weight, he would face co-morbidities (presence of two or more diseases) such as diabetes, heart disease, high blood pressure, or even cancer.

I was protective of him and didn't want anyone saying or doing anything to him that would hurt his feelings. The battle I fought within myself was great.

"What is she doing with Dr. Rosser? It must be because he is a famous surgeon; surely she doesn't love him…look at him." Those were the kind of remarks I would encounter during our courtship. I was even accused of being a "gold digger" who dated Butch because he was a surgeon. After all, how could I possibly find someone that large attractive? Butch was a well-respected professional in the community. He was a world-renowned surgeon with a down-home demeanor…not your typical doctor. Maybe in a way, people were protecting him. He was Akron's pride and joy.

Because I was known in the community for modeling (tall, skinny, attractive), I think people automatically assumed I had an ulterior motive and that was disappointing and upsetting to say the least. Growing up, my mother had always instilled in me and my little sister, Dawn, to always be able to take care of ourselves no matter what and we both did. I worked three jobs while attending the University of Akron. Upon my graduation with a business/marketing degree, I landed a corporate position at BF Goodrich (Geon). I worked my way up from customer service rep to being one of the first African American women sales reps in that company. I traveled all the time and enjoyed the relationships that I established with my customers. I had my own place, corporate car, expense account, and most all my freedom to experience life.

So, as an independent woman, I resented others thinking I would try to take advantage of someone because of their perceived fame and fortune. Such attitudes made me angry and sad. How could people be so shallow? How could they think that about me? The accusations and speculations were all new ground for me and slowly chipped away at my spirit.

Despite the naysayers, Butch and I continued our courtship. We truly enjoyed each other's company. He made me laugh like no one else. We opened each other's eyes to new adventures. Butch was always reluctant to try new things because of his weight and being self-conscious, and I was the total opposite. I would try something new every day if I could. Butch was not one to take risks unless it involved medicine/surgery.

How Excessive Weight Affected Our Attitudes Toward Life

Butch is a pioneer in the world of laparoscopic surgery and I admired that about him. However, in other areas, Butch was like clockwork. He would go to the same places because he felt safe, until he met me. In a way, I buffered the fear of the unknown for him. On the other hand, Butch broadened my horizon about things that interested him. We would go to art museums, car shows, and most of all, he taught me how to dream. Butch would often tell me stories about growing up in Mississippi without a whole lot to do but dream and read encyclopedias. He is one of the smartest people I know. I could ask him almost anything and he would know the answer. We have this joke that he is a human encyclopedia. However, don't ask him where his keys are because he certainly couldn't tell you. I guess you can't have everything.

As time went on, I could always sense when Butch would feel self-conscious about his weight. Considering he was reminded *every day* that he was different, he rarely expressed his feelings or fear while in a certain situations. However, his body language and his posture screamed *"fear."* This fear involved people's judgments, stares, lack of consideration, and most of all, empathy for someone who was different and struggling. Because I loved him so much, I felt what he was going through. I would even try my best to run interference if I could so that the blow society had for him wouldn't hurt so badly. For example, when I would accompany him to certain conferences and we flew domestically, I would make sure that we sat next to each other so he would feel at ease or I would ask the ticket agent to make they put a seat between us for his comfort. Butch usually took up at least a seat and half when traveling in coach. Clearly that posed an issue for the person sitting next to him.

There were times that we couldn't change seat assignments, and he took up half of the seat of the person next to him. Butch would always be so apologetic to them and most of the time, the people were kind and said it wasn't a problem. Then we would encounter those people who, when Butch would walk down the aisle, did not want to give him eye contact because they secretly prayed that "this big guy" would not sit next to them. In a way, I do understand. If you paid for a ticket, you should be able to enjoy the entire seat and not half a seat because the person sitting next to you is extra-large. Still, when it's someone you love, the rules or the tolerance change a bit. That's why, more times than not, I would sit with him. Honestly, I was uncomfortable, too, especially if the flight was full and I was in the middle, but I would do anything to buffer the pain that I knew he was in because of his disease. Little did I know I needed someone to help me "buffer" my emotions in dealing with what felt like endless travel challenges.

Butch would always have to ask for a seat belt extension because the regular seat belt would not fit around him. Most of the flight attendants were discrete about handing the seatbelt extension to him, but there were some that you can tell disdain bigger people and would say out loud so everyone could hear, "Here's your seatbelt extension, sir." Butch was embarrassed and so was I. It's like all eyes were on you, and I hated that. When things like that would happen, I could instantly tell Butch was super sad. I hated for my love to feel that way. Why can't people be a little more tolerant or a little bit more sensitive to people who have a weight challenge?

Another obstacle that Butch and I would encounter were the tray tables. Because Butch was so big, he could not let the tray table down. In my own little way, I would always make him feel like that was no big deal. He used my tray table, which of course I didn't mind, but I know that hurt him. He felt like he was inconveniencing me in some way.

Butch and me on New Year's Eve (1993) before we were married.

I would crack a joke and try to get his mind off of the many land mines that we encountered while traveling. When he wasn't traveling with me, there were times that he couldn't eat because he was sitting next to a stranger and he had no place to put his food because he wouldn't dare ask a stranger if he could share their tray table. When he would tell me that, it would hurt me so much. Traveling was so stressful for both Butch and me. Trying to keep him upbeat, running interference for his challenges, and taking on society's disdain for someone who is bigger was too much for me to bear at times.

I don't think Butch knew how all this affected me, and I dared not mention it to him. I was his biggest fan and cheerleader, so how could I tell him that this weighed on me, too? Pardon the pun. By the time we would get to where we were going, I was a ball of nerves. Working overtime to protect him from the prejudice of the world while at the same time trying to protect him from himself (self-sabotaging thoughts), and pretending to myself that none of these challenges bothered me was too much. I needed help, too. I wished someone would have noticed the toll all this took on me and once ask me, "How are you handling all this?" I wanted to scream, "I'm feeling anger, frustration, fear, and most of all—ashamed of all those feelings!"

Looking back on this experience, I guess I may have been an enabler in some form. I wish someone had told me that I was not the manager of the universe, and I couldn't control what happens to Butch and the world around him. All I knew was I loved him, I wanted to be with him, and I would protect him at any cost...even if it meant losing my sanity.

I remember one time when Butch and I were in the elevator, and it stopped at the next floor to pick up a gentleman. As the man entered the elevator, he unashamedly gawked at Butch and his size. His look of disdain felt hurtful. He didn't even say, "Hello, how are you?" He was just plain rude. Then his gaze changed as if he thought one of us might be a celebrity. That one minute on the elevator felt like an eternity. It was so uncomfortable.

At that point, Butch blurted out, "Yeah I'm her bodyguard and you're standing a bit too close."

Then we proceeded to exit the elevator at our floor. We laughed so hard because you could tell the guy tried to figure out who I was as the doors closed on him.

At times, I found myself looking for people looking at us when we were together. I wanted to somehow stare them down, so they would feel embarrassed and stop gawking at us before Butch caught them. I know this was sick. Were there times that I thought I wanted to run away from Butch and this whole situation? Absolutely! However, the love I had for him would not let me. Being with Butch was an adventure, to say the least, on many different levels. The one thing that was constant was our willingness to fight for our relationship—that was non-negotiable.

Anxiety happens when you think you have to figure out everything all at once. Breathe; you're strong; you got this. Take it day by day.
-Karen Salmansohn

Ask Yourself...

- *How do you feel about the way others look at and talk about your obese loved one? Or, about your relationship with that overweight loved one?*
- *What are your greatest fears if you were to talk honestly with your obese loved one about his or her weight and the challenges or issues obesity raise in your relationship?*
- *Does your enabling or protecting actions help or hurt them? Explain.*
- *What challenges have you faced in public with your obese loved one? How did those challenges make you feel?*

Would You Take These Actions?

- Write down some of the ways you try or words you use seeking to protect your overweight loved one from others hurting him or her.
- Write down the personal feelings you have never shared with anyone about your loved one's obesity.
- Has his or her obesity affected or lessened your love or caring in your relationship? If so, what will you do about the harm obesity is inflicting on your relationship?

-3-

STUMBLING FORWARD

The relationship was getting serious for Butch and me. I felt we needed to get counseling if we planned to take our relationship to the next level. After all, Butch had been married before with three children, and I had my own issues, so we thought it would be advantageous if we tried to work out the kinks before we said, "I do." I had already been in counseling prior to meeting Butch. I was counseled by one of the assistant Pastor's (Michael Henderson) at The House of the Lord (THOTL) about once or twice a month. I was reluctant to even start counseling because I didn't want everybody in my business. I didn't want the stigma of being crazy or mental.

Growing up in my household, getting help or going to therapy was never discussed. I felt like it was perceived within the African American community as a sign of weakness. Little did I know those counseling sessions helped shape who I am today. Being able to be "real" with Pastor Henderson validated my self-worth in a way that I can't explain.

I grew so much during those sessions and spoke so highly of Pastor Henderson to Butch that he said, "Wow, I would love to talk with him, too."

That was music to my ears. A man, a doctor nonetheless, open to counseling was a miracle. Most men I know would be reluctant to open up about their feelings and shortcomings to anyone—especially a pastor. Butch's openness to want to get better and want to make our relationship stronger was definitely a move in the right direction toward matrimony. It didn't hurt that

Pastor Henderson was so easygoing and personable. It was effortless to open up to him without feeling judged.

> **Counseling isn't a sign of weakness. In fact, going for help or counseling takes courage, strength, maturity, and self-awareness along with a willingness to grow and change.**

Our counseling sessions with Pastor Henderson went well in the beginning; like a honeymoon period, if you will. We discussed my fears of becoming a "stepmom" to Butch's kids and the challenges that come with being married. As the sessions went on, the topic of Butch's weight and health would take center stage and needless to say, it wasn't pretty. I had real concerns in regard to Butch's health. I had learned from my previous sessions with Pastor Henderson that I needed to speak the truth in love no matter how hard it was—stumble forward in a sense. I guess in a way, I found the courage to speak my truth about how his condition affected me, especially while Pastor Henderson refereed our lively discussion.

Pastor Henderson always knew how and when to ask the right questions and to bring us back to the real reason we made the commitment to come to those sessions. We both knew we loved each other, and we wanted to improve and mature in our relationship. Butch often felt Pastor Henderson and I ganged up on him, but to the contraire, Pastor Henderson was "for" both of us. He demonstrated that time and time again. I think it was so painful for Butch to look at this issue straight on with no way of escape that he became intimidated and quite frankly, scared. However, I knew if we were to make this commitment of marriage to each other, we had to tackle the issue of obesity head-on. I could not move forward without facing it. We didn't have to solve it completely, but we had to address it and come up with a viable plan.

Frankly, I was afraid for his life! I didn't want him to die as I had already faced abandonment issues from my childhood.

My mom and dad divorced when I was fourteen, and it devastated me. I totally felt abandoned. So, the thought of marrying someone whom I loved and then having him die or leave me was scary. I wanted to help Butch through this process. I never ever gave him an ultimatum that said he had to lose a certain amount of weight. *Never.* Of course, it was clear he needed to lose weight. I simply wanted him to go to the doctor to get a physical and get checked out. We would come up with a plan from there.

Surprisingly enough, Butch did not suffer with some of the co-morbities (hypertension, diabetes, cancer, etc.) many people his size were challenged with. However, Butch did suffer with sleep apnea, knee problems, and severe varicose veins. In my heart, I knew it was only a matter of time before his condition would worsen. A person can't continue to carry that kind of weight, deal with the pressures of being a surgeon, travel internationally, and think his obesity would not affect his health.

Butch's sleep apnea was one of the biggest concerns I had. Sleep apnea is a potentially serious sleep disorder in which breathing repeatedly stops and starts. Butch snored loudly and had excessive daytime sleepiness, which are two main symptoms of sleep apnea. There were times that I feared for my life while he drove. He would be driving on the highway; we would be having a perfectly normal conversation one minute and then the next minute he would dose off. I would scream loudly and get so mad at him for scaring me and nearly killing both of us. I would often offer to drive, but he was such a gentleman I think he felt bad that I had to drive.

As a doctor, I knew he knew he had sleep apnea, but I believe he was so afraid to find out the truth that he ran from it. Butch did not take care of himself; that was clear. Here he was a "healer" who could not heal himself. I know that had to weigh heavy (pardon the pun) on his heart. We had several discussions about his condition and my request for him to go to the doctor or sleep lab, but he was reluctant to take action and that angered me. I loved him and I desperately tried to help him. I would become so upset because I felt like he wasn't trying to help himself. ***I often wondered if he secretly wanted to die.***

Denial of the truth or facts about our health can damage our relationships with God, others, and ourselves.

For the next two and half years, our relationship continued to blossom. We both agreed to continue with pre-marital counseling because we felt we had a vast number of issues (work, parenting, health, self-esteem, relocating, etc.) that we needed to work through. We were committed to the process, even if it meant traveling to Baltimore to meet with Pastor Henderson who had recently moved to that area. We had built a rapport with Pastor Henderson, so we decided to follow him for our counseling sessions. That was dedication at its finest. If that wasn't enough, Butch was blessed to be offered a position at Yale School of Medicine in New Haven, Connecticut, which put yet another obstacle in our relationship: long distance. Through it all, we didn't waiver in our resolve to both get better so we could love each other the way we both deserved to be loved. I believe Butch knew I loved him and had his best interest at heart, so he did decide to go get a checkup. Now, that was a big step in the right direction. At that moment, I knew we would be all right.

On December 9, 1995, Butch and I wed in front of 300 witnesses; we made our commitment to God and to each other. I had a dream wedding. Everything about it was perfect even though it was one of the coldest days of the year. My heart was warm with great possibilities for the future. I remember Butch being so happy that day. As he waited for me to enter the sanctuary, people told me how he was beaming and interacting with the crowd. This was a new beginning for both of us. I do remember the challenge of obesity reared its ugly head with my handsome groom. Butch was self-conscious about the tux he chose to wear. He wore a white tux, one that he had custom made. He kept mentioning to me that he couldn't believe he chose "white" because it made him look even bigger than he was. He was a great sport and took the million wedding pictures, but I felt "the stronghold of morbid obesity" trying to take away the joy of that day. We both fought to not let that happen—not this day. I told him that I loved him and no matter what he wore, he was still my *boo*...my handsome groom.

Our wedding day (Dec. 9, 1995)

Life was like a whirlwind after Butch and I got married. Instantly, I became a stepmom to three beautiful teenagers, and I gave birth to twin girls in October 1996. That's right, five kids in less than a year. I also moved twice in that year, and Butch launched a new surgical center at Yale University. Thinking back on this time brings on stress. If that wasn't enough, I had to quit my job (job didn't transfer), and used to depending on someone else to take care of me.

That was a **big** challenge for this independent woman. Living in the northeast was definitely an odd experience for this midwest girl. Back home in Ohio, I was so used to saying "hello" and giving eye contact and a smile to strangers, but that was not the usual and customary gestures in the east. I definitely had to get used to that. On top of all that change was the constant, gnawing reminder of Butch's weight and my concern for his health.

> *I did not realize how deep my concern had become until I noticed I cringed every time the phone rang. I wondered if the person on the other end of the line was calling to tell me my husband had collapsed of a heart attack.*

Like most other morbidly obese Americans, he tried diets, pills, exercise, and fasting. You name it, he tried it, and nothing seemed to work. As if his physical suffering was not enough, I witnessed firsthand the emotional and social suffering he had endured from his colleagues. I think some of his colleagues were flat-out jealous of his accomplishments in the surgical world, so of course what better way to try to knock him down a peg than to prey on his weakness—his weight. Butch is a pioneer and innovator; he has always been one step ahead of everyone else.

"He doesn't look like a surgeon," some would say. Okay, what does a surgeon look like exactly? It's almost as if they totally discounted his abilities based on his physical appearance. Day in and day out, my hubby had to fight this battle and constantly overachieve to prove them wrong. This caused more stress, which made him eat even more. Food was his drug of choice. It soothed his soul and made the world easier to deal with, if even for a moment. When he would have these eating binges, I would get so mad! To myself, I said, "Stop eating! Can't you see this is killing you and me and allowing 'them' to win?"

I cannot imagine how painful it was for Butch to endure the cruelty of others, because watching it happen to him was painful. In fact, I had what I call, "sympathy pains." I literally felt like I lived with obesity without carrying the weight. I began thinking as he thought. Food became the highlight of our conversations. I remember eating when he would eat, even when I was not hungry. Butch always seemed to brighten up when we discussed food or were around it. Since I liked to see him happy, I would oblige.

We did not do the things I liked to do because Butch physically could not do them. I did not realize I was not living with a weight challenge the way Butch was, and therefore did not have to deprive myself of the things I liked and was physically able to do. Sometimes, I actually felt like I became Butch to a certain extent, and lost Dana. Instead of being myself, an outgoing, fun-loving, active person, I subconsciously took on the Herculean task of suffering right along with my husband.

He felt so judged; Butch was much more comfortable at home, in familiar surroundings, than having to deal with the stares, snickers, and downright rude people. Butch's weight prevented us from participating in many social events as a couple. I always wanted to go to the theater, to see plays and concerts, but we were unable to because Butch could not physically fit in the seats. Since I genuinely loved my husband's company and would not enjoy myself without him knowing he was home because of his weight, I would not go either. Was I angry and disappointed?

Yes! It was heartbreaking. I totally resented him. I'm not 460 pounds, so why am I suffering? I know you are probably asking yourself, "Well, why are you complaining? You knew he had this issue before you married him!" Of course, but I absolutely knew I loved him as well. I needed to find a way to cope, to be honest with myself and a trusted friend on how some of these obstacles made me feel. That is why I felt the need to write this book. I wanted to help the next person going through this.

As the result of loving an obese person, depression, anxiety, and panic attacks became my new reality.

I finally had to ask myself, *How can you help your loved one if you can't help yourself?*

Understand, I always thought I helped Butch. What I did not realize was that by not taking care of myself, I actually hurt him. Like so many spouses/loved ones of the nutritionally challenged, I suffered silently in many hidden ways. Too afraid or ashamed to admit to my feeling of anger, resentment, hurt, fear, sadness, disappointment, loneliness, and frustration, I stuffed them deep down inside myself.

I set myself up for total dysfunction and, eventually, a meltdown. Butch was not the cause of all my internal pain. I clearly dealt with my own individual issues, but facing this *huge* challenge simply compounded my afflictions.

Ask Yourself…

- *What are your fears regarding the person you love who is obese? (Check all the fears that apply.)*
  That person might die.
  That person will be hurt if I speak the truth in love to him or her.
  That person may reject what I share or abandon me.
  That person could _____.

- *When your obese loved one denies the truth about their obesity and its real or possible consequences, how do you feel? (Check all the feelings that fit you.)*
  Rejected
  Ignored
  Unloved
  Hurt

Fearful for him/her and me

Undervalued

Demeaned

Like a nag

Irritated

Frustrated

Desperate

Like a failure

Want to run away

Stressed

Worried

Depression

Despair

Hopeless

Negative and critical/judgmental

Anxious and worried

Lonely

Unloved

Sad

Disappointed in my loved one or myself

Other:_____

Would You Take These Actions?

- Are you willing to go to counseling? Are you willing to go together or by yourself if necessary?
- What are you doing to take care of yourself physically, emotionally, and spiritually? What will you start doing to care for you?
- If you shared the lists you checked above with your overweight loved one, how would he or she respond?

- Is there a friend of the same gender you can share your feelings with? If so, will you reach out? When will you?

Sharing More Family Pictures...

Our older children, (1995)
Duane, Nikki, Kevin

Dana with the twins (1996)

Butch with the twins (1996)

-4-

OBESITY 101

W e all know it is no secret that obesity is at epidemic proportions. More than one third of US adults are obese and childhood obesity has more than tripled in the past thirty years. What is going on and why is this happening to our society? We, as a society, are consuming too many processed foods and our portion sizes are out of control. We have become a more sedentary society with TVs, computers, smart phones, texting, and social networks, that occupy our time, so it is easy to forget to get up and move. What about the argument that obesity is a **disease** and should be treated and respected as such?

Did you know in the United States, sixty-one percent of adults are considered overweight? Of that, twenty-seven percent or 50 million people are obese and the number of adolescents (ages 6-11) who are overweight has tripled. The University of Colorado reports thirty-three percent of all women and twenty-five percent of all men in the US are on a diet.[3] They are not on one diet; they are resorting to special diets like Weight Watchers or fad diets. Dieters often jump from one diet to another as well. They haven't discovered how to take control of their health or their weight, so they try every new "diet" that comes along. Guess who is watching these adults struggle with their weight? You guessed it; our children.

> Obesity in one or both parents probably influences the risk of obesity in their offspring because of shared genes or environmental factors within families" (Whitaker, Wright,

Pepe, Seidel, & Dietz, 1997). The notion that "obesity
runs in families" has been supported by cross sectional and
longitudinal studies (Gibson et al., 2007; Maffeis, Talamini,
& Tato, 1998; Schaefer-Graf et al., 2005; Wang, Patterson,
& Hills, 2002; Whitaker et al., 1997). These studies provided evidence that parental overweight (defined as a BMI
≥ 25 kg/m^2) and obesity (defined as a BMI ≥ 30 kg/m^2) are
significant risk factors for overweight in their offspring.[2]

However you choose to view this epidemic, there is one thing that is
clear to me: whatever affects one person among our family, friends, and communities affects all of us. Obesity has been silently creeping into the family
dynamics for years and somehow we have been caught unaware of its deadly
grip. Obesity has run rampant for a long time and it's not until the last decade
that people are becoming even more aware of it. Would we know obesity is an
epidemic if the CDC didn't inform us of this fact? Would we know it was an
epidemic if it wasn't reported on the news or if the First Lady hadn't brought
her childhood obesity initiative ("Let's move") to your attention?

I think we are so desensitized to overweight people in general it has
become the norm. Isn't that scary? Our society has become unaware of obesity
as we go about living our daily lives. We are being desensitized to this deadly
disease and what it's doing to its victims and to their families and friends that
dare to love them. If the obvious health risks of being obese were not enough
of a daily fear for the family, there are unexpressed ailments that the families
silently suffer with that no one seems to acknowledge or address—until now.

The CDC doesn't report the millions of loved ones who support those
who suffer with obesity/morbid obesity and the monumental challenges they
deal with on a daily basis. They don't know how lonely it can be to hold feelings of anger, resentment, embarrassment, and the daily fear of losing their
loved one. Then they beat themselves up because they dare to feel that way.
It's not reported in the news about how the family dynamics change when we

have an obese loved one who can't participate in simple, daily activities with their children due to their physical limitations. Nothing is said about how our loved one can sometimes choose to become reclusive because of the way society treats them.

People who are not sensitized to this struggle don't know how it is to take on the responsibility of being their protector because of all the stereotypes and abuse they experience every single day. They want so badly to have a truly honest conversation with their loved one about their weight, but the fear of hurting their feelings overshadows the burning desire of the truth. Yes, this deadly disease is not just killing millions of Americans who suffer with it, it is infiltrating our families and we have to do something about it.

Dana's Point of View

Growing up in a predominately African American community, it wasn't unusual to have relatives, loved ones, or friends all around me who suffered with obesity/morbid obesity. It was a way of life, my reality if you will. It never struck me as a "bad" thing, and I certainly never thought about what their families experienced because of their weight challenge. As a child, no one in my immediate family suffered with obesity, so I had no reference point of the up close and personal struggles. I did have aunts or cousins who had weight issues. When our family would have family gatherings or reunions, being overweight wasn't discussed as a family. Rarely would I hear certain family members talk about a relative's weight.

A handful of times in my childhood, I may have heard a family member whisper, "You know Aunt Mary really needs to take that weight off," but that was the extent of the conversation. No one ever teased anyone or in my eyes made the obese relatives feel less of a person. Obesity was all around me. At church was the worst. There were so many overweight men and women—especially women—that it was the norm. It was often looked upon as a badge of honor in a way. The bigger you were, the better it was eluded that you could sing. Everyone knew the bigger the church cook was, the better the food would taste, especially the fried chicken and pound cakes. No one wanted a skinny cook in the kitchen. Remembering this makes me sad in a way. Again, we judged someone based strictly on their appearance. So, a thin person couldn't cook? Really? How narrow-minded is that?

I researched Overeaters Anonymous and discovered unlike AA, there are no support groups for the spouses of obese family members or friends. So, I became even more determined to develop support, help, coaching, and equipping resources for people like me! That's why I am writing this book. I discovered my story as a spouse living with an obese person connects with others in my position. Let me share with you two stories that you may identify with in part. These are real people (names have been changed) sharing their personal stories.

Sometimes life's challenges and painful experiences can teach us lessons that we didn't think we needed to know but needed to feel.
-Unknown

Lauren's Story

I want to start by thanking you for giving me the opportunity to express my feelings about this subject. By coming forward with my story, it is at least temporary therapy for me, but if I'm able to help someone else, then this is all worthwhile.

I married a good man! The first time I saw Daniel, with his slender physique in a navy blue suit carrying a beautiful butternut briefcase, I thought to myself, "Who is that?" And then I answered myself, "That is going to be my future husband." No kidding! We had met through a blind date and the rest is, as they say, "History!" When we met, I was literally blown away with his style, charisma, intelligence, and most importantly, the relationship he had with his mother. As the old saying goes you can tell how a man will treat you by the way he treats his mother. He was everything any woman would ever want in a man. I didn't know underneath there was a hidden battle he had fought all his life and that I was going to be fighting that battle alongside him for many years.

The battle is obesity. I am not good at guessing one's weight, but I do know Daniel wore a size 32-34, when I met him. I can now honestly say without hesitation he is probably wearing a 54, easily if not more. I would never ask him, because in this household it is so taboo. As I sit here, I have so much to say regarding this sensitive subject, but I find myself speechless from the guilt that has weighed so heavy on my heart for so many years. I have tried everything in my power to help my spouse. I truly felt I could change this problem by supporting him and working together. So many times we put together a workout regimen and a complete healthy eating plan, but shortly afterward, I would find myself working out alone and seeing the signs of closet eating. I would not wish this on anyone's relationship.

Daniel and I have been together now for over fifteen years and maybe three years of our relationship I would label "normal." When I say "normal," I mean doing things as a couple, things as simple as social gatherings, being with friends and family, and going to church. This obesity problem has changed our whole lifestyle. When we married, I vowed that the things I did before we got married wouldn't stop, but my spouse's weight problem has been all-encompassing.

Daniel is filled with so much shame that he has isolated himself from everyone and everything. All our friends have the utmost respect for him; they wouldn't dare say anything regarding his weight. They love him very much, but they too have seen the cycle for many years. The only safe place for him is around food, and eating, too, is done alone.

A healthy lifestyle is what I live for! I avidly workout four to five days a week; plus I add extra things in between. Eighty percent of the time, I eat properly and the other twenty, I treat myself for all the hard work and dedication I've put in. I cook for the week (in hopes) that my spouse will eat the same as I do, but seventy-five percent of the time, he isn't interested. Yes, the dishes are mainly "vegetarian," but there are so many great, healthy, meatless dishes out there!

My feelings are tearing me apart. When people ask where Daniel is, I always have an excuse why he isn't present. When I see other couples enjoying one another, I feel so sad! Does he even care about my feelings?

I lie in bed at night and ask the Lord to please help us. I pray, "Help him get his weight under control; don't take my loved one away due to health issues." I know the Lord doesn't work on my time, but when is He going to knock on our door?

Daniel is now on medication for diabetes, but doesn't take it consistently. If something happens, I will feel so responsible. Every day when the phone rings I pray it isn't that call. Every morning I wake up and hope nothing happened to him during the night as we slept. In my heart I know it's just a matter of time before I get that call and I will question myself, "Was there anything more I could have done?" How can you help someone that doesn't want to help themselves? They see and know the consequences, they know the strain on the relationship it has caused, have they given up? Should I?

When I finally have the courage to bring up the conversation about his weight, my heart is pulsating and I feel like I'm walking on eggshells. Not in fear of anything violent, but in fear of hurting his feelings. My feelings are being hurt everyday by seeing what has occurred in our relationship. I have suggested weight loss programs such as Jenny Craig and Weight Watchers or hospital weight management programs at numerous facilities. Although I personally think those programs may only be quick fixes, I also feel something is better than nothing. But as *time goes on and the weight increases, he feels so hopeless. I wonder if he thinks he can't dig himself out of this overwhelming situation. Then I wonder if he is "willing" to put in the work to dig himself out. I know just how far to take the conversion before one of the following happens: he either shuts down or leaves the room. What is a person to do? To a certain extent Daniel knows how I feel, how can he not? However, it continues to be the elephant in the room.*

This whole experience has been like a cycle. There have been many times throughout our marriage that he's had things under control. Life was good during those times. I was so happy! Daniel is so gifted with many talents; one is his voice. He has a beautiful voice! I have envisioned him so many times in our church choir just belting it out! I see that special glimmer in his eyes when he hears a certain song. It gives me goosebumps! He used to lead in the choir. His self-esteem was through the roof during these times! He is also such a "people person!" When he walks into a room, you can feel the energy filled with magic and excitement! You are drawn to him like a magnet! But when the "other person" decides to visit, it cuts him off from everyone and everything and his only way to survive is work.

Over the years, I have learned there is never a good time to bring "it" up. It is like walking on crushed glass in your bare feet...painful. If there was one place as a family he would join us is at our holy home. We both grew up in the church, and we love the Lord. When he does, I hope and pray it is not too late.

This problem has affected our marriage immensely. I do everything alone unless I'm accompanied by family or friends. I'm now used to it. I have gone so many years being upset that it no longer hurts as bad. Until you have walked in these shoes, you will never know how both spouses end up suffering when one is fighting this disease. How can I go on living like this?

I must admit it has been almost a year since I started my story. Things have not much changed since then. In fact, if anything, it is far worse, and I am sorry to say, I can no longer take it anymore. I wish I could end this with a fairytale ending, but that will not be the case; I am done! I would never wish for anyone to live this way as a couple. I have been alone for many, many years.

Sarah's Story
Living and Dying with Obesity

No one knows more than me about living with obesity because I was obese and so was my husband. For me, being overweight was my problem. Not anyone else's. Now that I have lived on both sides of the fence, I'm sure that's not true. Obesity affects everyone in the family. I never thought much about how my being obese affected my family, but in hindsight I know it did.

I wasn't always obese. I, like many women, began to gain weight after marriage and babies. After my second child, I ballooned from 160 to 240 pounds. My husband never complained about my weight, and while I knew I was bigger, no one in my family brought it to my attention. In fact, I didn't realize I had increased my weight so much until I received a picture of myself in the mail. This picture shocked me! I had no idea that I looked so big. I thought I had put on a "few" pounds, but not to the point that I looked fat. That day I went on a weight loss program and began my journey to regain my life back. Unlike many people, I was fortunate not to have obesity-related health issues, but that was not the same for my husband.

When I met Walter, he liked my girlfriend. I thought he was a nice guy, but she was not interested in him because he was overweight and she was not attracted to him. At that time, Walter was morbidly obese, weighing 300 pounds. He and I became friends and before I knew it, we got married. At that time, I didn't care that he was obese; what was on the inside was most important to me. He was kind, loving, and hilariously funny. It wasn't until a short time after we were married that I realized his weight was a problem for me. The main problem was I wasn't attracted to him sexually. His stomach and the fat around his pelvic area shrunk his penis, which didn't satisfy me. Prior to that, I never gave any thought that the stomach is sitting smack dab in the middle of our bed. But it was there and it affected our sex life.

The biggest problem is Walter has suffered from high blood pressure and diabetes since he was in his mid-twenties. Walter's biggest love was food. Food made him happy! *He enjoyed not only eating, but cooking. He was the best cook. He also loved to entertain. We would have gatherings at our house and Walter loved to prepare the food. Don't get me wrong; I love food, too. So I did not help when it came to keeping things healthy. I have come to realize we were very much egging each other on. In fact, I think we used each other as a reason to eat. In other words, I could eat whatever I wanted and so could he. After all, how could I influence him to make healthy choices if I wasn't making them myself?*

That all changed in 1998, when I received that picture in the mail that showed me how fat I had become. I was mortified and I immediately took a drastic step and went on a program at a local weight loss center to lose the weight. Three months later, after seeing my progress, Walter joined me. By January 1999, we had lost over 150 pounds together! That's an entire person out of our bed! Sexually, we came together like we never had before! Our passion was ignited and for the first time in ten years, I was actually physically attracted to my husband. Life was great! Our story was featured in Ebony *magazine.*

But as the saying goes, all good things must come to an end and they did. In 2000, we relocated from Texas to Florida where I began a stressful career under less-than-ideal circumstances and I began to eat my way through it. I regained all of the weight I lost and then some; and so did Walter. I was upset and disappointed we had let ourselves go. I also was disappointed Walter was never a support for me. It was a case of "monkey see, monkey do" and unless I followed through, he wasn't going to either. I needed him to support and encourage me, but he never did. I think he was relieved not to have to follow the program. In my case, I hated the way that my husband relied so much on me to motivate him; I needed help, but he was oblivious. So we both let ourselves go and it was a disaster!

By 2004, I weighed 250 pounds and Walter had blown up to 270 pounds. Worst yet, Walter was on six or seven medications, including insulin. At first I didn't realize he was taking so many meds because he would hide them from me. I would find the insulin in the refrigerator in the back, hidden behind food. He didn't want me to know his condition had worsened to the point of using insulin. The effect of so many medications became evident in the bedroom. He was impotent and it affected our sex life. He started taking erection dysfunction medications, which ultimately affected his heart. We ended up in separate bedrooms and our marriage suffered greatly.

I remember when Luther Vandross had his stroke. Walter and I watched him on Oprah and I begged him to do something about his health because I knew that was where Walter was headed. He used to get so upset with me when I would bring up his weight. It was an off-limits topic and I believe he resented me for bringing it up. I made several attempts for both of our sakes to get back on our original program, but we could not get our acts together. I would cook a healthy meal and he would eat out. I would get so angry I thought, "If he doesn't care, neither do I. It's not my responsibility to take care of him."

In March 2004, after numerous attempts to get the weight off, I took a drastic step and had gastric bypass surgery. When I was going through the informational sessions for the surgery, one of the statements they made that "went one ear and out the other" is that the divorce rate for those who have the surgery is around eighty-five percent. I never thought that would be me. I was wrong.

After losing over 100 pounds, I regained my confidence. I looked and felt good. My husband was not. His health got progressively worse, but he preferred to go on more medications than to change his diet. Now don't get me wrong—he attempted to lose the weight, but he would not stick with it. He was in serious denial. Surgery was not an option for him because he would have to be 100 pounds overweight. I would ask him to go to the gym with me and to eat the meal plan I was on, but he wouldn't. We grew apart.

In 2007, for many reasons, we separated and in 2008, after eighteen years of marriage, we got a divorce. In hindsight, I realize he slipped into a depression and was immobile. I could not believe the statistic caught up with me. I thought my marriage was stronger than that. It wasn't. To this day, I wish we had both made better choices.

I wish that Walter made better choices so that his health hadn't declined. I wish I wasn't focused on my sexuality and stuck it out to help him make better choices. If I had, then maybe he would still be alive today. After our divorce, Walter's health continued to decline. He lost his job and health insurance, and a month later, he lost his life. Sadly, when cleaning out his home I found several "off limit" foods for someone with his health issues. Until his death, he was still in denial.

Through this experience I have learned obesity affects everyone around you. Even if your family does not complain about your weight and how it affects them, it does affect them. No one knows more than me how hard it is to lose weight. I have fought the battle for twenty years and still to this day, continue to fight. My daughter, who has 100 percent of my husband's genes, is obese. The sad thing is, even after seeing what our family has been through, she does not want to do anything about her weight. This helps me to realize if it does not come from within, nothing will change. There has to be something to make a person know enough is enough. The question is, when is enough, enough for you?

Now you have read some of my story and those of others. Let's move forward together to understand how we, as loved ones, can help ourselves and our obese family members.

Ask Yourself

- Am I willing to research more about the health-related and relational problems associated with obesity?
- Will I start telling myself the truth about my situation? What is the reality of my life as I am living and relating to my obese loved one?
- What negative emotions and behaviors are emerging in my life and our relationship that have roots in the problem of his/her obesity?

Would You Take These Actions?

- Write down your story like the stories you have just read.
- Write down the emotions and behaviors that need to change in you. Remember, you cannot change other people, but you can change yourself. Is there a friend who can support you in reading this book with you and helping you change? Will you ask them for support?

-5-

"It's Okay; I Know How you Feel."

"It's okay; I know how you feel." How wonderful those words could have comforted my soul from a trusted friend or family member. It would have been wonderful to know I was accepted in spite of what I felt. I asked myself:

- *Is there anyone out there who truly knows the challenges that a loved one goes through when faced with obesity in their family?*
- *Has anyone ever stopped to think we exist?*
- *Had anyone ever felt what I felt?*

I did not have the guts to truly admit to myself, let alone to anyone else, what I had secretly gone through. Even now, writing about the feelings and challenges I had is hard for me. Whether you are the spouse, family member, friend, or even the one who is challenged with their weight, I want you to know every time I wanted to give up writing this book, your faces kept popping up in my mind. I saw the faces of those of you who are lovesick for the wellbeing of your loved ones.

How's the Communication Between You and Your Loved One?

Facing the challenge of obesity everyday can be heart-wrenching. I wanted to see my husband healthy and happy and prayed for him (and me) daily. On one hand, I wanted to somehow forget about the challenges. Nonetheless, I was constantly reminded of the reality of his obesity through his physical disabilities, unwanted stares from cruel heartless people, health issues, the media, and the list goes on. I struggled with "coming out" about my feelings because of the fear of being judged. I asked myself (as you may be asking yourself):

- *Do I love him?*
- *If I love him then, why do I have these negative, hurting feelings?*
- *I certainly would not be ashamed, right?*
- *If true love is speaking the truth in love, then what do I fear?*

Communication is verbal and nonverbal. Facial expressions, tone of voice, touch, body language, the way we dress, and even silence all communicate our feelings to others.

I have learned loving communication is clear, consistent, caring, continual, and confrontational.

Clear: You don't have to be a doctor, scientist, or nutritionist to share information about the health dangers of obesity or the realities of how you feel, as long as you take responsibility for your feelings and refuse to blame others for the way you feel. Don't say, "You make me feel ashamed, worried, anxious, etc." Instead, say, "I choose to feel _____." Remember feelings are real, but not reality. You can face those feelings and make choices about how to respond to your loved one in healthy and caring ways.

Consistent: Stop changing your mind and being indecisive with what you are communicating. Be consistent in speaking the truth in love and stick with the same message. Don't be an emotional rollercoaster. Stick with the facts and the truth.

Caring: You are speaking truth in love because you care. If you didn't love your obese family member or friend, you would not be sharing the truth. Remember, the person isn't the problem and is not defined by the problem. They have issues and need your help and support to face reality and solve problems.

Continual: Don't give up. You may feel overwhelmed, helpless, or hopeless. The only way you can fail to make progress is if you quit and give up. One bad day doesn't erase the good days you have. One step back doesn't negate the steps forward you are making. Stay focused and on course with your continual communication of the truth in love.

Confrontational: Confrontation doesn't need to be negative, angry, argumentative, condemning, or critical. You can speak the truth in love, offering positive options for moving forward through the challenges of obesity. Ignoring the problems and repressing your feelings will only grow festering anger, bitterness, and resentment in you. Don't fear rejection. Your loved one may reject what you are saying, but that does not mean they are rejecting you. You are loved by God and others, so hang in there.

Supporting someone with a nutritional challenge can bring up a lot of complicated feelings that are difficult to articulate. You have fear, which is an acronym for *False Evidences Appearing Real.* I was constantly afraid that because of my husband's weight, he might have a heart attack, die, and leave me. Did it happen? No, but I was afraid of it. I was afraid of the world—how cruel and heartless people can be to the obese. I feared Butch might fall asleep while driving and kill himself or someone else due to his sleep apnea.

Obesity is the Enemy, Not Your Loved One

Living with anxiety and fear day in and day out was so hard for me. Fear literally became my shadow. I love my husband so much. I love his laugh, smile, wit, intelligence, the way he cracks me up, and his boldness. I absolutely think he is adorable. I could go on and on. I always felt like I had finally found someone who accepted me for me. I was afraid I would lose him to *obesity! How dare this disease take him away from me. Obesity is the enemy, not Butch.*

I was so mad at morbid obesity. What does "morbid" mean? The definition of "morbid" is, "suggesting an unhealthy mental state or attitude; unwholesomely gloomy, gruesome." "Obese" is defined as, "very fat or grossly overweight." Now put the two together. In layman's terms, you could say "morbidly obese" means "gruesomely fat." How would you feel if someone came up to you and said, "My, you're gruesomely fat"? That feeling that you are experiencing right now (if you have a heart) is how I feel about those words. It is demeaning and gives a sense of hopelessness. I know morbid obesity is what the medical community defines as "extremely overweight," but it doesn't make me feel good nonetheless. What I am trying to express is how all aspects of this disease affected me.

"The Nutritionally Challenged"

Doesn't that sound more powerful? Everyone involved in this issue can feel like, "Yes, it is a challenge, but a challenge that can be overcome. This contains the possibility for hope and winning instead of losing and dying." I needed help from someone who had gone through this thing. I needed help from my Almighty God. However, when you feel like you are on an island with no help in sight, you rely on what has been comfortable for you. In my case, I took the wrong path of denial, ignoring the challenge, and being too proud to admit I needed help. At times I was angry, sad, ashamed, vulnerable, scared, happy, and filled with a multitude of contradictory emotions about what this disease did to my family and me.

I know you are probably thinking, *you had feelings of happiness regarding this struggle?* Yes, I did. I was happy when Butch had decided to work on his weight, whether it was in the form of diet pills, exercise, healthy eating, etc. I was happy to work out with him, take on a healthy eating challenge; whatever it was, I was happy to do it. Then, the happiness led to frustration when I would see him slip right back into some of the same unhealthy eating habits. I couldn't control the highs and lows of my feelings. Instead of being proactive with my feelings, thoughts, and decisions, I was reactive. I was on a roller coaster of emotions, which were reactions to what he did. Instead of making healthy decisions about my feelings, thoughts, and actions, I simply reacted to him. *Stinking thinking,* as Zig Zigler used to say!

Instead of being *reactive*, become *proactive*. Make your own healthy decisions on how you will respond to a loved one who is nutritionally challenged.

I would react with happy feelings and begin to hope whenever he would take a step toward health. I would daydream of simple things that I wanted to do with him. For example, when we would go to the movies, we would usually have to sit with a seat between us for his comfort, oh how my soul ached. I wanted to sit next to my sweetie, smell his popcorn-laden breath, kiss his cheek, and snuggle under his neck like most couples do.

You may say ask, "Dana, why are you complaining? Didn't you know this before you married him?" Yes, I did and I never once thought because of the temporary inconvenience of his weight that I wanted to jeopardize the love I had found in him. Make no mistake: I loved him no matter what. If he never ever lost one ounce, I would still love him the same. Yet, because I loved him so much, I wanted to share as many precious years as I could with him. I knew when a person carries such excess weight, the odds are not good for a long and healthy life. I would fall into the pit of constantly thinking, *I'm going to lose my precious husband.*

I Needed Someone with Whom to Share My Emotions

The biggest problem for me was being able to find someone that I could truly share my feelings with. I was bursting at the seams. If I truly communicated what I thought and felt to my spouse, I ran the risk of hurting his feelings. After all, I never wanted to be perceived as one of those fat-hating people, because I'm not. I am a good woman praying and hoping to extend the life of my spouse. Am I different from anyone else who wants to help his or her loved one? Are you any different than me in this regard?

I felt if I shared my true feelings with my loved one, another family member, or even a trusted friend, I would be burned at the stake for how I felt. Where does that come from? Aren't there people out there who want their spouses to stop smoking, gambling, or abusing drugs? Of course there are. Don't these individuals seek help in dealing with their loved one? Of course they do. Then why is it in my mind that it is so taboo to talk about this challenge? People already thought I married Butch because he was a surgeon and had a hidden motive. So, I stayed silent about my feelings because I did not want to give people any reason to think their assumptions were right, even though Butch and I knew the truth.

Unexpressed emotions will never die.
They are buried alive and will come forth later in uglier ways.
-Sigmund Freud

Disneyland Dilemma

Almost every kid and adult has a deep desire at some point in their life to want to visit Disneyland. The Rosser family was no exception. As a kid, I had always dreamed of entering that magical world of never-ending attractions and fun. At the time, the twins were around three when Butch and I decided to take them. Beyond excited was an understatement when we told them our plans; they couldn't wait to meet Mickey, Minnie, Goofy, and to see Cinderella's castle. I must admit I was excited as well, but a little apprehensive about the amount of walking Butch would have to do, if the size of the rides would accommodate him, and if he would tire out and want to go back to the room. I wasn't sure how that all would work. I did know in my heart that he wanted to go and experience Disneyland, so that is what I was going to try to concentrate on.

Upon our arrival, the kids wanted to go everywhere and ride every ride. I needed to temper their enthusiasm. For one, I knew we couldn't see and do everything in one day. As much as I didn't want to admit it to myself, I also knew Butch would be limited as to how much he could walk and participate. Looking back on this situation now, Butch and I should have discussed some sort of contingency plan in the event that he wasn't able to keep up with the pace of the day. For me, for once I wanted to feel "normal" without having to constantly be concerned with his challenges. Knowing that wasn't totally realistic, I still pressed on to do everything possible.

Because of my secret apprehensions about Butch's challenges, I tried to avoid rides and steered the girls toward all the other million and one things to do at Disneyland. They had their faces painted, played games, saw shows, and went in search of characters throughout the park. Butch always cracked jokes when we would take pictures with the characters. He is a clown; I so love that about him. Of course, as fate would have it, we could only avoid the rides at an amusement park for so long. I tried to keep everyone happy, except I forgot one person: me. I wanted the girls to have a good time while also trying to avoid the inevitable pitfalls I knew we were about to face with Butch. This juggling act was terribly draining, however, I was determined not to be robbed of my Disneyland experience.

As Butch and I approached the ride that the girls begged us to get on, I could feel my heart racing and my stomach doing flips. Out of the corner of my eye, I could see Butch sizing up the ride to see if it would accommodate his frame. As we sat down on the ride, it appeared all was well with Butch. He fit in the seat, and I instantly felt a sense of relief that we would have at least one successful ride with Daddy.

While we got settled, I noticed each passenger had to put on their seatbelt for safety precautions. As Butch pulled his seatbelt around his waist, it would not buckle. He tried and tried, but it was not long enough to accommodate him. My thoughts screamed, *"No!* Please God, *no."* In my "I can fix everything mode," I had wondered if amusement parks had seatbelt extensions as many of the aircrafts we had flown on had, but I feared asking. There were scores of people in line waiting for their turn, and they have quick turnaround times for the rides, so I knew that would not be an option.

As the operator walked around to make sure all the passengers were securely locked in, I wanted to curl up in a ball and roll away. I knew they would not allow Butch to ride if he couldn't fasten his belt. As the operator approached Butch, he quickly realized his seatbelt would not fasten. The operator had no choice but to tell Butch he would have to get off the ride if he could not fasten his belt.

As Butch got up from the ride, the twins cried, "Daddy, where are you going? Come back! We want you to ride with us."

I felt like my heart broke into pieces and fell all over the floor. If that wasn't enough, I knew he felt embarrassed to have to walk past all those people because they all knew why he had to get off. I mouthed to him that I loved him and swallowed all of my feelings. I was embarrassed, angry, sad, and most of all, ashamed for feeling the way I felt. I longed to get off that ride and hug him, but I now had both of the girls that I had to see after. Our babies had no idea why Daddy couldn't ride. They totally didn't get it. They kept asking me where Daddy went. I remember telling them that Daddy's seatbelt was broken and he couldn't ride without it. It took every fiber of my being not to totally breakdown in front of them.

I honestly tried to enjoy the ride with the twins, but I kept thinking about how Butch was doing. How did he feel? Did he want to go back to the room after this incident? What kind of mood would he be in? All I knew is I needed to be brave for everyone, the question was, "Who was going to be brave for me?"

Confronting the Shame

Shame is a terrible gnawing feeling. Dr. Brene Brown, in her book, *Daring Greatly,* defines shame as, "the intensely painful feeling or experience of believing that we are flawed and therefore unworthy of love and belonging." Everybody has experienced some form of shame in their lives. Shame is one of those things that no one ever wants to talk about.

Shame would eat at me like cancer ravages through the body. Every time I felt it, I would get another dose of shame on top of the anxiety I already felt. Layers and layers of shame are a recipe for disaster that led to a depression that took over my body. I don't want anyone else to have to suffer through that. Are you ashamed of your loved one's weight and pretending you aren't? If you are ashamed, why do you feel that way? Are you embarrassed at his disabilities because of his weight? Are you angry with your loved one because they cause you not to be able to do things you would like, and then feel ashamed you feel that way? I have been through all these feelings and scenarios. They are real and more importantly, hard to admit. I guess that is why I am writing this book. I feel God wants me to set somebody free by saying there is no need to hide anymore.

This chapter is designed to let you feel whatever it is you feel without being judged. It's one that needs to be exposed so the journey will be a little easier to travel. I think I am also opening the eyes of those who are struggling with obesity as well. I know my husband had no idea all I went through. Butch told me that if he had known, he would have wanted to share the burden. So, by exposing these issues, it may enlighten those with a weight challenge to understand their weight is not affecting them personally, but the whole family.

Being a True Friend

The common denominator in a true supporter of a nutritionally challenged loved one has to be a foundation of unconditional love—for your loved one, yourself, and your family. Hiding and being dishonest with your feelings will start to bleed into other areas of your life and cause you additional drama and trauma. By getting it out, you are able to "exhale" what you feel and move on. Hiding and holding your feelings inside can cause you stress and limit your ability to be a good friend.

People who are nutritionally challenged need you to be their friend, whether you are a spouse, sibling, child, or loved one. They need your "friend stamp" of approval first before they can open up and truly trust you with this difficult challenge. In being balanced, healthy, and proactive, we can encourage them to be the best they can be. Isn't that the ultimate goal we want for them?

Ask yourself...

In a diary, notebook, or journal, write down your responses:

What I would like to say to my loved one about my feelings about their weight is _____

_____

_____

The ways our relationship is affected by their nutritional challenges are ____

_____

_____

The ways my loved one can support me are _____

_____

_____

_____

What are the three most embarrassing situations we have experienced as a result of being nutritionally challenged? _____

_____

_____

Would You Take These Actions?

- Share what you have written above with your loved one.
- Write a statement or thank you prayer about all the attributes and actions of your loved one that you are thankful for and share this with him or her.

-6-

INTIMACY

I know intimacy is a tough subject to tackle, but I am prayerful I can express my feelings in a way who is tasteful and informative. First of all, it is no secret that having a partner that is morbidly obese creates intimacy issues. People who don't have weight issues face some of these same challenges, though maybe in different ways. Yet, it is seen as taboo or distasteful to bring it up. It seems to be okay to discuss it if your libido is out of order, but if you have excess weight that causes intimacy problems, it appears uncouth to talk about it. I remember finding out that people would talk behind my back and speculate on how we "did it." I am still trying to figure out why anyone would sit around and meditate on the position we would engage in to make love. What they insinuated was the real issue, though. Because Butch was so large, they wondered how we were able to "connect."

There is so much more to love making than "connecting," but clearly there may be some issues in this area. Anyone who knows Butch knows what a passionate person he is. He is a huggy, kissy kind of guy, and I love that about him. He is passionate about his work, his cars, and of course, me. I always felt Butch loved me unconditionally, which was something that was foreign to me. I had never experienced that level of love before in my life. No matter how I acted or behaved, he was always there with open arms to accept me back. When it came to intimacy, Butch was no different. He would truly worry about my needs before his own.

However, I began to feel like he did that because he may not have felt he deserved to be "loved" because of his weight. Times when I would try to show him love, it seemed he could not fully accept it, which in turn made me feel bad. I wanted him to know I loved him for him. I married Butch knowing he weighed 460 pounds, but he would still act so ashamed and shy with me. Butch was so much more to me than a 460-pound man. He was a superhero in my eyes. I knew he knew my heart and my adoration for him, but it jfelt like it was not enough to help him overcome his own inhibitions.

Trying to Show Affection

Trying desperately to show my affection, and then get rejected time and time again began to take a toll on me. It got to the point that I did not want to initiate intimacy because I did not want him to feel bad. He was always thinking during our intimacy moments. Eventually, it became a distraction for both of us. Now, I know what he was thinking, but back then I did not. He worried about things like:

- Was his stomach too big, was his weight hurting me, and did I find him repulsive?
- I knew he wasn't all there emotionally, but what's a girl to do when you want your man? Frustration is not a good component during times of intimacy.

Did I want my husband to lose weight and have more confidence in himself? Sure I did. I wanted more than anything for him to be healthy. Of course, the byproduct of his weight loss would be for him to be in better physical shape. Who wouldn't want their spouse to feel and look the best they can.

However, if Butch never lost a pound, I would love him the same. One point I have to communicate here is how important it is t*o let your spouse know without a shadow of a doubt you love them no matter what.* If you are feeling like you have fallen out of love with them because of their weight gain, then maybe it would be best to bring in a third party to discuss your feelings. Truthfully, I would have to wonder if the problem in your relationship is the weight or if it is something more serious. I certainly don't have all the answers, but I suggest you should not be afraid to seek outside counsel if it is needed to reestablish a healthier relationship.

One of my goals in writing this book is to help couples, families, and friendships confront and survive every challenge. Society is so into, "if it doesn't work, throw it away and get a new one," that it has taken a serious toll on all levels of relationships. Not happy with how you look? Then get a new body, get a new face, get a new stomach or get new breasts. Things not going well on the home front? Then get a new home or a new spouse. The job no longer fulfilling and satisfying? Get a different job, go to a different church, and the list goes on and on.

What you must understand is when you get a new spouse, friend, partner, or any other relationship, there can and probably will be just as many issues, if not more, than in the previous one. There is a saying, "the grass is always greener on the other side." I would say don't be fooled; it could turn out to be AstroTurf!

Advice

1. Love each other unconditionally.
2. Put the other person's needs first.
3. Share openly and honestly.
4. Pray with and for each other.

Ask Yourself...

- *What is working well in your sex life?*
- *What challenges do you both face?*
- *Are you willing to share with one another how you both feel?*

Would You Take These Actions?

- Discuss any limitations your partner's weight has on your sex life.
- If you have lost that loving feeling, are you willing to talk with a counselor about your challenges?

-7-

BY ANY MEANS NECESSARY

"Girl, I think you are pregnant; something is not right with you, and I'm buying you a pregnancy test right now!" my sister blurted out to me.

I had to step back and look at her like I thought she actually had a point. She noticed I had been on edge and mean, which is totally uncharacteristic of my normally happy-go-lucky demeanor. In turn, I thought she was getting on my nerves, which now that I think about it, she normally doesn't do. So, I thought there was no way that I could be pregnant so soon after my marriage of only two months. I had been diagnosed with endometriosis about eight years prior to my marriage, and I felt the odds of me getting pregnant so soon were slim to none.

Endometriosis is one of the most common gynecological disorders, affecting over five million women in North America alone. Endometriosis occurs when the endometrial tissue that grows inside the uterus, grows outside the uterus—on the ovaries, fallopian tubes, and other areas in the pelvis. The breakdown and bleeding of this tissue each month can cause scar tissue called lesions. Although there is no cure for endometriosis, there are several treatment options such as surgery, medications, and hormone therapy, of which I experienced all three. Even though Dr. Moretuzzo, one of the best OB/GYN doctors on the planet, told me the odds were good that I could get pregnant after my last surgery, I still felt the one thing I had always prayed for (children) would be a dream deferred because of this voice in my head that told me I didn't deserve of such a blessing. So, pregnancy could not possibly have happened so fast!

Obviously, God had another plan for me. As I stood with my sister in the bathroom reading the positive results of the pregnancy test, I knew my life would never be the same. Not because of the obvious change of being pregnant and having the pleasure of assisting God with this miracle of life, but also with the realization that my prayers had been heard. Thus, I was deserving of happiness. If that wasn't enough, soon after I found out I was pregnant, I also discovered I was carrying twins! Wow, they say children are a gift from God, so this meant He loved me. I felt this was God winking at me and showing off how much He loved me. That is how I will always choose to believe this miracle.

After the initial shock wore off, I started all the mother-to-be rituals such as eating right, exercising, taking my vitamins, and experiencing the weird cravings. I craved fruit like crazy, especially anything citrus. I would eat pounds and pounds of strawberries, blackberries, cherries, and grapes; you name it and if it had a citrus taste, I would devour it. Butch found himself craving fruit right along with me which was weird, because he never was a big fruit fan. Butch was over the moon with excitement about the arrival of our bundles of joy. He had been married before and had three children, so the pregnancy experience was nothing new for him. I think Butch started thinking more about making changes with regard to his weight once he found out we were pregnant with twins. Wanting to be around for these babies seemed to be a motivating factor in him seeking out ways to lose weight and to enjoy a healthier lifestyle.

Because of this, I think he was in a position to accept the fact that he could not handle his weight challenge alone and he needed help. So, when we met with a close friend of the family and saw how much weight he had lost with the help of a weight loss facility called, "Structure House," I think a sense of hope was ignited in Butch and the possibilities of leading a fulfilling life sprouted in his spirit like a beautiful spring flower.

Structure House—Hope for Change

Structure House is one of the leading residential weight loss centers and fitness spas located in Durham, North Carolina. So, when Butch talked to me about going, I was so excited for him and encouraged him to go for it. I even asked him if he wouldn't mind me going with him so I could be right by his side. At first I don't think he could believe I wanted to go because I was pregnant and with twins. However, I looked at Structure House as a great way for both of us to learn about healthy living, through diet, exercise, the psychology of obesity, enablement, and how to develop new insights, attitudes, and behaviors.

So, off we went on another Butch and Dana adventure. Butch and I always enjoy each other's company. We like traveling to new places together, and this was no different. We arrived at the Structure House campus, a bit apprehensive about what to expect. I wondered if the room would to be big enough, if the bed was king size, and would it be sturdy enough. I had major concerns of how far the facilities were from our room because I knew Butch would get winded if he had to walk too far.

I even worried about whether or not Butch would like the food. If he didn't like it, I wondered how I would survive ten days with a mad man. Butch loves his food and he can get very when he is hungry. So, knowing our carb intake probably would be cut substantially did not give me a warm fuzzy feeling. I certainly prayed we could tolerate this whole Structure House experience without the drama.

Nonetheless, I was excited about learning how to cook healthier for all of us and I looked forward to finding an exercise regimen that we both could do together. I never wanted him to go through this journey alone. I knew I would be the main one preparing meals and buying groceries. So, the more knowledgeable I was, the more successful we would be.

Upon arrival, we checked in at the main building in which we received our room assignments and schedule for the week. The main building reminded me of a hotel lobby. We didn't know what to expect, but I didn't feel any weird vibes from Butch as we checked in. It felt like I was continually checked him out—quizzing him on his feelings, energy, hungry levels, etc. Even to this day, I often ask him, "Are you okay; is everything all right?" I can't help it.

Some of the residences at Structure House did give me the look like, "What are you doing here?" At the time I probably weighed close to 200 pounds, not bad for a pregnant woman of three months carrying twins who stood 6"2." In a strange kind of way, I felt like the "odd" man out. Everyone else there was fairly heavy. I did notice I told everyone I was three months pregnant with twins. Maybe in some crazy way that would make me feel more accepted, because after all, my tummy was expanding rapidly. I wanted to be like everyone else for these ten days and feel a common bond with them. Before I got pregnant, I thought I could stand to lose fifteen pounds, but this experience was not about me. It was about Butch and wanting him to feel as comfortable as possible, even with me.

When we arrived in our room, I was pleasantly surprised. The room was spacious and more than adequate for both us and oh yes, the bed was fine.

Taking Care of Him While Ignoring Me

The next couple of days were filled with exercise classes, counseling sessions, cooking demonstrations, and getting used to eating healthy. My level of fitness was pretty good at that time. I usually exercised at least three times a week, so the exercise classes were not that challenging for me, even being pregnant. During the classes, I would observe Butch and how he struggled to do the moves, but my soul was hopeful because he was there, trying to do better, wanting to learn. That was a huge step in the right direction for our whole family. Even though he may not have been able to keep up with the steps or moves, I could tell he felt safe. He was in a place where no one judged, stared, or made him feel less of a human being. After all, everyone was there with the same struggle and that made it easier somehow not to be perfect. Instead of always making everyone feel "comfortable" with his size and his bigger-than-life persona, he could finally concentrate on "Butch the man" trying to get healthier.

The one obstacle that I noticed throughout our stay was Butch's lack of flexibility. If we had to do an exercise that called for us to get on the floor, I would immediately get nervous for him. I knew if he got down on that floor, he would have trouble getting back up. Butch's knees and ankles seemed to be a point of contention for him all the time. The body was not meant to carry 450+ pounds and his knees would remind him of that constantly.

It seemed like he always twisted his ankles with the least turn in the wrong way. The awkwardness in which he got up from the couch or chair added to his chronic injuries. Butch would have to turn completely around with all of his weight contorted on his left foot for balance, while twisting into a push-up stance to get up from the couch. Every time he would do this kind of "acrobatic" move, I knew he felt terrible because people would look at him like, "What in the world are you doing?" The things that normal-size people take for granted like standing straight up from a chair, tying one's shoes without assistance, or being able to fit comfortably in an arm chair is an everyday struggle for those who suffer with their weight.

I never wanted Butch to feel embarrassed in anyway; so unbeknownst to him, I would fret and internalize everything while constantly asking myself, *What if he falls, slips, twists his ankle, or starts breathing too hard?* You name it, and I was worried about it. I prided myself on being his protector even amongst our allies at Structure House. I often wondered if I truly protected him or was I protecting myself? Did I not want people looking at me with embarrassment or shame or was it Butch? Honestly, I think it was a bit of both.

> **I would often get the "poor pretty woman stuck with the fat man" stare from people; it made me so mad and sick to my stomach.**

Those people didn't know Butch or me, so how could they judge our situation? Why did they assume I was stuck with him? Did they ever think I loved him? Were people even thinking those thoughts or did I make this all up in my head? I tell you, all of this thinking, worrying, and the "what ifs" were so exhausting, there was barely enough time for me to take care of myself being pregnant with twins.

Our bodies are capable of anything.
It's our minds we have to convince.
-Unknown

Surviving on 1000 Calories!

Eating at Structure House was an experience to say the least. I believe I had to be on a 1000-1500 calorie a day diet. Hello? You got a pregnant woman with twins here! So, after I informed them of my bundles of joy growing in my stomach, they quickly increased my calorie intake. I was so happy, I didn't know what to do! After that calorie increase for me, the people who lookedat me with the "What are you doing here?" stare, now envied me because I got more to eat then they did. Talk about feeling like an outsider! For the most part, though, the residents at Structure House were friendly, warm, and engaging people. They were easy to talk to and extremely open about their struggle.

There were several obese couples there which I found to be interesting. I often wondered if, at first, one of the spouses was obese and then, as a result, the other spouse picked up weight, or had their weight struggle brought them together somehow. I know for me, there had been times that Butch's fixation with food would rub off on me. He would be eating something late at night and even if I was not hungry, I would eat right along with him because the food kind of brought us together. There were times Butch would be eating breakfast and talking about what he would eat for lunch. I would ask him, "Why are you worried about your next meal?" Yet, I picked up that pattern of thinking about the next meal myself which lead to me putting on a little more weight.

I didn't even realize I engaged in bad eating habits until I stepped back and analyzed how my patterns started to emulate Butch's. The food at Structure House left a lot to be desired. It wasn't that the food was terrible; it was more about how my body craved salt and sugar. For me, mealtime wasn't something I looked forward to and maybe that was their strategy.

**Instead of living to eat,
we were learning to eat to live.**

Butch surprisingly didn't complain too much about the taste of the food; it was the portion size that he had an issue with. Soon we got used to it, especially once we saw how the weighing scale worked on our behalf as we began losing weight. At the end of the first week, Butch lost thirteen pounds, and

I lost ten pounds. That was an awesome feeling. I did, however, worry about the babies and if I gave them enough nourishment and calories they needed. In spite of our weight loss, the low sodium, low fat, and small portions got to Butch and me, so one day we decided to "break out" and leave the campus for the evening. Even though we could leave the campus any time we wanted, we kind of felt guilty we did not stay and stick it out with our peers and endure dinner. We both fantasized about "eating on the outside," and at this point, any restaurant would do.

Believe it or not, we strayed off campus to a nearby Red Lobster. I remember looking around in the restaurant to see if any staff members or patients from Structure House were in there ready to catch us red-handed. Butch and I surprisingly did not go crazy with our food choices. I believe we ordered broiled fish and vegetables, but I do remember we ate those oh-so-tasty biscuits they provide with your salad. After our sinful rendezvous, we headed back to Structure House feeling guilty. I should have been strong for Butch and not given in to the temptation. He needed me to be that pillar of strength, but my taste buds and babies screamed for "real" everyday food.

Going There Was a Big First Step Toward Health

For the next several days, Butch and I continued to go through the program. We attended counseling sessions, group meetings, group exercising classes, and cooking classes. They armed us with all kinds of skills and information to follow once we returned home. I knew this was a good start, but deep inside I knew when we got back home, Butch would not follow the program. His schedule at that time was so busy, and he traveled extensively. With that type of inconsistency in his life, I knew it would be hard for him to eat right and exercising would definitely be a challenge for him.

There were even times at Structure House where he missed classes because he was in the room working to try to meet the endless deadlines he was under. I would get mad because the purpose of that experience was for him, not me. He would justify his actions with the same old, "I gotta get this done."

Don't let the stresses and busyness of life distract you from what's important—a healthy lifestyle.

I wanted to say to Butch, "You gotta get your life on track before it's done; that's what you need to do," but instead I kept quiet. I also knew Butch would make excuses because he felt vulnerable. The exercises and activities were challenging for someone his size, and I think he didn't want to feel like a failure, even among his peers. He didn't miss a lot of classes, but I wanted him to get the most he could out of this experience. I knew in my heart that this would be a journey for both of us, but I was at least comforted that he had taken a first, significant step in trying to get his weight and lifestyle under control.

Ask Yourself...

- *Have you taken the initiative to learn about nutrition and healthy living?*
- *Would you be willing to adopt the "any means necessary" concept for your loved one?*
- *Have you noticed a change in your eating habits?*
- *Do you think your loved one would consider a weight loss facility? If so, would you go to support them?*

Would You Take These Actions?

- Explore a healthy living lifestyle.
- Consider taking a healthy cooking class, subscribe to healthy living magazines, etc.
- Take care of yourself (body, mind, and spirit).
- Exercise, do yoga, hobbies, worship, or meditation.
- Be mindful when you are hungry. Don't be swayed into bad eating habits.

-8-

A Family Affair

After much prayer and concern for Butch, I interviewed our family members about their attitudes toward his obesity. Why? Because the spouse, close loved one, or friend is not the only one affected by the nutritional and health challenges posed by a morbidly obese person. The attitudes of other family members can significantly uplift and support or damage and hurt both the overweight person and those trying to support and address the challenges of obesity.

So, I have summarized from my interviews the attitudes and relationships of the following family members with their approval. After you see how I have approached this subject with those connected to or related to my husband, perhaps you can develop some ways to approach, understand, and even elicit the support of those in your family. First, I will summarize each person's attitudes and relationship, then I will offer some advice at the end of this chapter in how to move forward with a similar, "Love you much meeting."

In the South, We All Like to Eat

Butch had a love affair with food; he talked about it constantly. Food is part of the Southern culture that he grew up in. Growing up in the south (Mississippi), food was and still is synonymous with love and hospitality. "Eat until you get enough, baby," is the mantra many Southerners profess. However, it's ironic that the hospitality food that is so generously offered to you can turn into criticism and taunting if you abuse it by becoming obese.

While our families rarely mentioned anything about Butch's weight, comments were made at times secretly, but never directly to him. Talking about being overweight in Butch's family was somewhat taboo. It was one of those unspoken codes. Butch was always so happy to see everyone, but he also anticipated his mother and sister's great cooking whenever we visited them in Mississippi. The food was indeed **amazing.** From fried catfish and chicken, greens, mac and cheese, pies, cakes, and sweet tea, it was a smorgasbord of heavenly southern cuisine. Butch would always put his food requests in before we got there and, of course, his mom obliged; he was her baby. Even though I believe they knew Butch was well over 400 pounds, they still fed him whatever he wanted. It was their love language. They didn't get to see Butch that much because of his busy schedule, so welcoming him home with all his favorite foods was what the "doctor" ordered.

Even the local gas station, called the Double Quick, prepared southern food in the store. You would go in to pay for gas and the aroma of fried chicken would be in the air. You had to get two pieces—you had to. It was so good, especially with hot sauce on it. Even though I didn't eat that much fried food back home, I felt like you were almost given a license to eat that way while in Mississippi. I did feel bad at times eating so unhealthily, but it was so good that I put it out of mind at times.

It was obvious this "Southern food thing" ran deep. One time, when we visited Butch's family in his hometown of Moorhead, Mississippi, I asked if they had any fruit in the house. They didn't, so I asked Butch to take me to the store to get some. Of course he said, "No problem Dana," but I felt a little uncomfortable about asking and I certainly didn't want to make anyone feel bad. Back home I didn't have a lot of processed food in the house, and I didn't cook the fried foods that Butch desired. It wasn't because I couldn't cook (I'm a great cook), but I knew it wasn't good for any of us. I always tried to help Butch with his weight in any way I could.

I never wanted to make anyone feel bad for what they ate, however, I wanted fresh fruit, yogurt, and cereal for breakfast. These were the kind of foods we were used to eating at home. Fried catfish, grits, toast, bacon, or sausage taste heavenly, but eating that way for breakfast everyday was too much for me. I wasn't used to it. When I ate like that, I felt sleepy after I ate breakfast even though we had just awakened for the day. For the most part, I learned to go with the flow and adapt to my surroundings. Because of this reality, I felt trying to bring up Butch's weight with his family may have been hard and possibly controversial, so unfortunately I never did. Looking back on it now, I wish I had tried.

Butch with his parents
(Mr. & Mrs. James Rosser Sr.)

Butch and his brothers (Chuck and Ludie)

Dawn: Working Alongside Butch in "Protective Mode"

Upon college graduation from Ohio University, Dawn Mitchell (my sister) was blessed to be offered a job at Yale University working alongside Butch as he launched the Laparoscopic Center. Butch was always big on helping family when and where he could. Butch's brother, Ludie, also worked with Butch at Yale, and his children have also worked on different projects there through the years.

Dawn was a laparoscopic coordinator and took care of organizing surgical programs, for the center. Dawn worked so closely with Butch and the medical staff at Yale, she witnessed firsthand how people whispered and talked about Butch's weight behind his back. Such talk would infuriate her and cause her to go into "protective mode."

"Protective mode" didn't necessarily mean Dawn would go back and tell Butch what people said about him because she didn't want to hurt his feelings. She candidly shared how she often felt like Butch's bodyguard, in spite of her petite frame and Butch being four times her size. She would stare people down who would gawk at him or snicker about his weight behind his back.

She tried to head people off before they would say or do something inappropriate with regard to Butch's weight. At times, she would scout out venues to make sure there would be chairs that did not have any arms which would restrict him from sitting comfortably.

As an international expert in the field of surgery, Butch was in high demand as a speaker. However, because of Butch's obesity, he suffered with sleep apnea which can cause excessive daytime sleepiness. Dawn always became nervous and anxious when it was time for Butch to give a speech. Butch would often dose off, even on stage, as he waited for his turn to speak.

When this happened, Dawn's anxiety level would go through the roof. She would sit in the audience praying he would wake up before they called his name to come to the podium. Ironically, like clockwork, Butch would miraculously pop up and give his speech beautifully, concluding with a standing ovation. Dealing with the ups and downs of his sleep apnea were, at times, too much to bear, especially riding with him in the car. Having to be on constant alert was exhausting, always fearing he would fall asleep at the wheel.

She often wanted to prove his naysayers wrong when it came to judging him because of his weight. One time, Dawn overheard other doctors talking about Butch's weight, saying when he applied for the position to Yale, he put on his application that he weighed 350 pounds, but everyone knew it was 450 pounds or more. She knew what they said was true, but it hurt because they came from a place of judgment, not one of genuine concern for his health and wellbeing. She wanted everybody to leave him alone and allow Butch to do what he does best—be an innovator and an amazing surgeon, helping and healing people around the world.

However, Butch's weight did concern Dawn deeply, and she felt he needed to get it under control for his own quality of life. After all, he was married to her sister. She cared for both of us deeply and wanted to see us have a long happy and healthy life together.

Dawn and I would often talk about Butch and his weight challenges. She was probably one of the only people who truly understood my day-to-day battle. She knew firsthand how difficult this was to deal with and was my confidant. I didn't have to apologize to her when I would get frustrated. I knew she didn't judge me for sharing with her my "real" feelings and wouldn't question my love for him or think I had a hidden agenda for marrying him. She knew I loved him and that made all the difference in the world to me.

However, even though I was blessed to have my sister in my life to share those "not-so-pleasant" experiences and feelings with, I still found myself "holding back." This holding back was not intentional. I think it was done subconsciously because these feelings were so deeply rooted and had been kept buried in this "secret" hiding place for so long, that I didn't even fully grasp or articulate the pain I experienced. It often felt like I couldn't get everything totally off my chest, even with my sister.

The sadness Dawn experienced in dealing with Butch and his weight added to my own sadness and I wanted to take her pain away. It felt like everyone around Butch experienced the pain of obesity and I didn't think that was fair. Honestly, sometimes after talking with Dawn, I was angry at Butch. How come he couldn't recognize the fight we all were in daily? I knew in my heart his fight with morbid obesity was much worse than ours, but we each had our own real and painful battles we fought as well. If he would have acknowledged our efforts or acted like he cared, that would have been some type of consolation for this daily fight.

Though I knew he dealt with his own pain, that didn't stop ours from stealthily progressing. What none of us realized at the time, though, was Butch had no idea how his battle with obesity affected those of us who truly cared about him.

Kevin's Summary

Kevin is the oldest son of Butch's five kids. As a young child, Butch was much like a superhero to Kevin. He saw Butch as larger-than-life and with superhuman powers as a doctor. It was rare to see a black surgeon back in the '80s, especially one with whom you could truly relate. Some of the parents of Kevin's elementary school classmates worked at the hospital with Butch and looked up to the Rosser family as a whole. Kevin was truly proud of his dad.

However, upon entering junior high and high school, Kevin started socially feeling the stress of Butch's weight. Kevin's peers went from admiring him and his dad in elementary school to feelings of envy and jealousy in junior high. Kids looked at Kevin and his "good life" with his doctor dad like that of the Cosby kids. A lot of the black kids perceived Kevin as thinking he was better than everyone else and started to tease him about his dad's weight because they knew it would hurt him. It was a living hell for Kevin. Kids would call Butch "fat ass" and say, "Your dad is big as hell."

At times, Kevin could not contain himself and would yell back at them, "Why don't you tease me and leave my dad out of this?" Kevin learned fast that the world was cruel to people with weight challenges. It especially hit hard when that target was his hero, his dad. To survive these attacks, Kevin had to learn the "fight or flight" response. Either he would run from the attacks or fight and stand up for himself and his dad—he chose the latter. In a way, Kevin felt like he got his "edge" back in junior high from defending his dad's honor.

In high school, Kevin was a great basketball player and his dad would support him at his games. Some of the players on his team came from broken homes and were a bit envious Kevin's dad came to support him at his games. Kevin looked up to his dad and talked about him all the time. In order to get back at Kevin, some of his teammates teased him about his dad and his weight. On one hand, they admired Dr. Rosser and looked up to him, but on the other hand they used his outward struggle against him to tease his son.

Kevin loved his father dearly, but because of this constant tug of war over his obesity, he also resented his father. Didn't his dad see what Kevin went through on a daily basis because of his weight challenge? Didn't he realize his bad eating habits contributed to his weight gain which in return caused Kevin to have to disconnect from his peers? The shame Kevin felt for feeling this way was unbearable. When Kevin would see his dad eat something that was bad for him, he would get infuriated and have to leave the room.

Kevin remembered sadly how his dad would always eat the kid's food off their plates at the table. "If dad asked for a bite of your food, it was understood he would eat half of it. No one dared challenged him or gave him the 'side eye.'"

According to Kevin, no one in the family ever addressed their dad's weight head-on. Kevin's younger siblings never talked about their dad's weight, even in private amongst themselves. They were all too afraid they would be overheard by their parents. The younger siblings also were affected by their dad's weight. Duane started to realize his dad's physical limitations in fourth and fifth grade, while Nikki remembers a time when it would take him a long time to get down the steps, and it would concern her. One time, Kevin overheard his mom defend his dad to others about his weight. Kevin was proud of his mom for standing up for his dad, just like he did in school.

Butch with Kevin and the twins (Taylor & Tianna)

"People would say negative things about my dad," Kevin remembers, but his mom would defend him and say, "Well, that **fat man** saved hundreds of lives this year."

After Kevin graduated from high school and entered college, the dynamics with his dad's weight changed a bit. The teasing from schoolmates subsided, but the constant gawking from total strangers would get to him. Kevin often found himself "mean mugging" people who would stare. This discomfort prompted him to walk behind his dad as if to make one believe he wasn't with him. The shame he felt for doing that was hard to take. He loved his dad, but the relentless judgmental stares were hard to bear at times.

One day, Kevin and I had a heart-to-heart conversation about Butch's weight. I'm not sure how the conversation started, but I was glad it did. We both poured out our hearts to each other. I felt so happy that he felt comfortable enough to open up to me. We both were concerned about his health. We talked about his sleep apnea, stress, and possible other comorbidities (diabetes, hypertension, high cholesterol, etc.) that could develop if he did didn't do something about his weight. Kevin was emotional during our conversation, which in turn made me cry. He had all this pent-up pain regarding his dad and he needed to get it out. Kevin shared how he wanted to talk to his dad about his concerns, but he was afraid and couldn't imagine how to even broach the subject.

Let's face it: who wants to talk to anyone about their weight, let alone their parents? I totally understood his fears. I reassured him that he was not alone in this journey and I would be right here with him every step of the way. We decided to even role play how he would approach his dad and how the conversation might play out. I played the role of Butch and kind of came off touchy and distant. It's interesting that my experiences with talking to Butch about his weight were not the same as everyone else's. It wasn't like it was a subject he loved to talk about, but as his fiancée at the time, he was a lot softer with me. I also knew he felt safe with me. So, I gave tips and insights to Kevin about how and when to approach Butch. Timing is everything and talking to him late at night after a long day of surgery was probably not the most opportune time, I advised him.

Kevin was prepped, but petrified to say the least, but one day he blurted out to Butch, "Daddy, I love you and I want you to lose weight. I don't want you to die."

He did it. He finally felt free from all the judgment and condemnation that he had inflicted on himself for feeling the way he did about his dad's weight. He mentioned to Butch that he and I had a conversation about his weight and I had encouraged him to reach out. Kevin started to cry, and surprisingly, so did Butch. Butch felt his oldest son's heart and responded with love and understanding. Butch tenderly grabbed his son's hand and sat with him in silence, taking in all that had been said. Now that's the true definition of bittersweet; a pleasant and painful experience indeed.

Behind the Scenes

In preparation for writing this book, I wanted to get other family members' opinions and vantage points for how they dealt with Butch's weight. To do that, I asked them if they would be willing to sit down and have an honest and open interview—no holds barred. After I set up a voice recorder with everyone's permission, we all sat around the kitchen table and poured out our hearts concerning this man we all loved and cared about.

Butch was not present which I feel was important. I wanted everyone to be open and honest and not feel bad, judged, or intimidated by Butch's presence. Everyone trusted me with their feelings and knew whatever was discussed, good or bad, would not be exploited or used against them in anyway. Initially, I prepared questions for the interview, but as the session went on, I didn't need them. Everyone fed off of each other. As the session progressed, more and more memories and feelings poured out like a faucet that had been finally allowed to flow unhindered.

Each family member was given the floor and simply asked to tell about their experiences with Butch. When we first started, there was a lot of nervous energy and we talked about anything other than Butch and his weight. Even though everyone agreed to the interview, when it was time to "get real" it was a little scary. Numerous times, I tried to get it going by saying, "Okay, y'all let's get serious." Digging up all those mixed feelings of hurt, pain, shame, and sadness was hard for all of us.

The first person to speak had the hardest job. I think everyone wanted to see how authentic and open they were expected to be before it was their turn.

Once we all got over our initial nervousness, the interview went smooth and effortless. Two hours later, when the interview was over, we all came away with a clarity that truly helped each of us fight for Butch daily in our own way, though he didn't know it at the time. He didn't know the ignorant people we kept away from him who talked about him behind his back, the many times we arranged special provisions for his size, the inconveniences we endured to make him feel comfortable, and the countless times we had to temper our own feelings of anger and frustration to protect him and his feelings.

The common thread with each interview was the concern for his health. We all shared times when we wanted to confront him for eating things that were bad for him, but had held our tongue. We wanted him to know we battled his weight problem right along with him, but somehow found it difficult to share this with him. We were warriors battling for him, but it didn't feel like Butch appreciated it. What we discovered through our sharing was he didn't know about our silent struggle because we had never openly talked with him about it.

Butch carried around 460 pounds worth of hurt of his own. Sometimes the one with the "main" struggle never knows how much sacrifice is made by his loved ones on his behalf. Once I told Butch about all things I battled, he was dumbfounded. He had no idea I had my own daily issues because of his weight. He told me he wished he had known sooner. Knowing I suffered right along with him could have been one of the motivating factors to help him achieve his weight loss. Hearing that, I wished I'd had the courage to be more open with him sooner. Please learn from my mistakes!

Ask Yourself...

- *Are you willing to talk about obesity issues with family members? Why or why not?*

- *What have you learned from my experiences in this chapter?*

Would You Take These Actions?

This dialogue among family and loved ones was helpful as it gave them a safe place to express their feelings about this real challenge in all our lives. Here are some helpful hints and tips for you to act upon in organizing your own, "Love you much meeting."

1. **Pray!** Ask God for guidance as you take on this task. It's not easy to open up and be real about a loved one's weight. Remember, this exercise is designed to bring freedom and even healing for you and your loved one. I promise, you will feel better once the meeting has been accomplished.

2. **Write** down your personal concerns for your loved one and what you want to get out of this meeting. The worst thing you can do is tap dance around your feelings. Be as open and honest as you can. Resist the feeling you are betraying your loved one by expressing yourself. Remember, this meeting is for you, but ultimately will help your loved one as well.

3. **Be selective** of the family, loved ones, and friends you invite to this forum. This is a touchy subject and the last thing you need is for someone to go back and misrepresent the truth to your obese family member. Select those family members/friends who have integrity and have shown a genuine interest in your obese loved one's health and wellbeing.

4. **Before the meeting**, ask those attending to write down their concerns, observations, experiences, and possible ideas on how to support you and your loved one.

5. **Set the ground rules and objectives** of the meeting. (For example: no bashing or teasing.)

6. Take notes or even record the session if everyone feels comfortable. I found it helpful after the meeting to go back and listen to what everyone had to say. I always pick up something I missed.

7. Gather the information you received and pray. Determine whether you will share about your meeting and feelings with your obese loved one or keep it to yourself. There is no shame in not sharing your feelings if you're not comfortable or ready. Just opening up dialogue about your feelings in a safe environment is a "big baby step" to your healing.

8. Resist feeling awful. No doubt this will be a hard exercise. Sometimes, we have to do those things that are hard for us in order to give birth to a new beginning. Take a deep breath and know you are worth it all.

-9-

LEADING WITH LOVE

"We need to talk."

Those are the four dreaded words that I know most husbands hate to hear from their wives. Usually, those four words imply they are in trouble or the conversation is going to last much longer than they would like. In writing this chapter, I started to think if I could pinpoint one conversation that I sat Butch down and said, *"We need to talk about your weight. We need to talk about how it's affecting me and about how it's affecting our family's quality of life."*

For the life of me, I can't pinpoint one essential and important conversation. Butch's weight was constantly on my mind, and I frequently brought up the "nutritionally challenged" issue *indirectly*. For example, I would make a comment about how people stare so much at us when we were out in public together. I would say, "Boy, people act like they haven't seen 'big' black people before." I would include myself in that description because I am a tall woman. However, I knew in my heart they gawked at Butch and his size. I needed to include myself in the description because I didn't want him to feel alone.

I always protected him and would indirectly talk about how I missed going to live concerts, musicals, and professional sporting events. My remarks would often be about the seats being uncomfortable. Now don't get me wrong, those seats were not the most comfortable just for someone who was 450 pounds. Theatre and stadium seating are notorious for being narrow. For a morbidly obese person, it is almost impossible to sit in most seats. I would bring up how I was concerned for his general health, but would never *directly* give him an ultimatum and say, "Look, you must lose weight," and then list the reasons why it was necessary and essential *now!* I knew this was a sensitive subject for him and it never felt like the right time to talk about it. Butch dealt with his weight every single minute of every single day. So, I felt he knew he needed to lose weight and didn't need me reiterating it over and over.

Their Obesity Challenges Us

As much as I tried to bury my feelings of concern, they always came out sideways in some form. I became moody and short-tempered with Butch and the kids, which was unfair to everyone.

My buried feelings of fear, anxiety, frustration, sadness, and anger would keep me from doing the things that were healthy for me—physically, mentally, emotionally, and spiritually.

I just existing, merely surviving. I didn't realize I had entered into an abyss in which I lost myself. Yes, I totally lost touch with what made up the unique individual named Dana. I allowed myself to become lost in the day-to-day routine of taking care of kids and worrying about my husband's health. I never stopped to think about what made life meaningful for me. There was simply no time.

Since I couldn't change the reality of my situation and I couldn't change my husband, I had to face the reality that the only person I could change was me! A Jewish psychiatrist who was imprisoned during the Holocaust could not change his situation or those around him. Victor Frankl came to this conclusion: "When we are no longer able to change a situation, we are challenged to change ourselves." My husband was nutritionally challenged; at the same time, my identity and meaning in life was challenged.

Anxiety and depression felt inevitable for me. I once read a Facebook post (Anxiety & I) that stated,

> Having anxiety and depression is like being scared and tired at the same time. It's the fear of failure, but no urge to be productive. It's wanting friends, but hating socializing. It's wanting to be alone, but not wanting to be lonely. It's caring about everything then caring about nothing. It's feeling everything at once then feeling paralyzed and numb.

This definition was enlightened me.

I don't want to come off like I'm blaming Butch for my state of mind because clearly it was not his fault. I lived with the choices I had made to bury my feelings, to deny reality, and to lose myself in busyness. He didn't fully understand the magnitude of how his morbid obesity affected me because I didn't communicate it fully to him. So, how can I blame him? He didn't realize I thought everyday would be the day I would get "the call."

"The call" was a morbid fear that I had rehearsed over and over in my mind, that his office would call me and tell me he had a heart attack or he had a car accident as a result of falling asleep at the wheel because of his sleep apnea. No one knew I was tortured with this constant voice in my head endlessly repeating for me the possibilities of his mortality. What about my mortality? Did I ever think of that? No, I never thought I could damage my own physical and emotional health with all those "what if" scenarios. I desperately wished so bad that I could talk to someone about how I felt without the fear of judgment. My questions may well be some of yours:

- *How do I even start the conversation with Butch about how I feel?*
- *Where do I begin?*
- *Will he get mad?*
- *If he becomes defensive or withdraws, will I feel rejected and responsible for putting up walls in our relationship?*
- *Does having negative feelings about our situation and his obesity mean my love for him isn't unconditional?*
- *Will he think I don't love him?*

What's Next?

In writing this chapter, it was so important to me to be able to give concrete advice on how to sit down and talk with your loved one about this sensitive subject—morbid obesity or being nutritionally challenged. I have thought long and hard about what advice I could give to that spouse, family member, friend, or colleague in confronting (speaking the truth in love) a loved one about their excessive weight. No one is comfortable with confrontation. It is much better to be authentic and express your true feelings with love than to have your spirit broken daily by the fear of the truth. The truth will set you and others free.

Below are some strategies that can be used when confronting your loved one about their weight:

1. ***Breathe and pray.*** Come up with your intentions. Pray and get guidance from God. Make sure your spirit is right and your intentions are clear. God will give you courage. Meditate on truths, not myths or fearful dreads of "what if he/she _____ (fill in the blank with all your negative outcomes)."

2. *If possible, have a support person (trusted and trustworthy friend) who will role play your conversation with you.* This could be a counselor or someone who has been through a twelve-step program like AA, OA, NA, or the like. Remember, "I" messages take responsibility for your feelings, thoughts, and behaviors while "you" messages often blame and criticize the other person. For example, instead of saying, "You being overweight makes me worry about losing you," you might say, "I worry when I think of the health problems being excessively overweight can lead to heart problems, diabetes, and cancer."

3. *Write down your concerns.*

   a. Get to the core of the issue (health, future, kids) with a clear, concise list. Writing a letter is another option.

   b. When you go to a physician with a health problem, you may often write down your list of symptoms. Likewise, make a list of your feelings, thoughts, worries, and concerns. Share that list with your loved one. Remember, you are taking responsibility for what you say. You are not blaming that person for how you think, act, or feel.

4. *Lead with love by confronting lovingly, speaking the truth.*

   a. Lay a foundation of love first.

   b. Sit down in a quiet, private place, facing each other and be aware of your body language. Don't cross your arms or scowl. Be open and casual, not closed and uptight. You are not disciplining your partner; you are sharing in a calm, concerned, and caring way.

   c. Be honest and speak from your heart. Don't be condescending or critical. Listen to their feedback. They may respond defensively, angrily, or unexpectedly. Paraphrase back to them what you hear them saying and the feelings you are observing that they have.

d. Have a calm, caring dialogue, not a monologue.

5. **Be supportive. Affirm to that person that you are on their team.**

   a. Affirm neither of you are "the enemy, obesity is."

   b. Let your loved one know you will support them.

   c. Ask them what they need from you to begin moving toward overcoming the challenge of obesity, morbid obesity, or being nutritionally challenged.

   d. Discuss how to recruit other family and friends to be a supportive group or team for both of you.

   e. Don't have a specific goal like, "You must do this or _____." Instead, discuss a variety of healthy options for moving forward.

   f. Let him/her know they are not alone—you, others, and God are there for them, love them, and desire health and long life for them.

6. **Let it go—being the authority figure.**

   a. Don't become the food police or raise your eyebrows.

   b. Always have your heart open.

   c. Your loved one may need time to process what you are sharing and consider the options of moving forward. Encourage them to talk to others—friends, counselors, nutritionists, physicians, etc., about their issues. Remember, your loved one may not want to do anything about it right now. Ultimately, they have to own their decisions.

When I shared these points with my husband (coming from the position of the nutritionally challenged loved one), he responded. Here are some of his thoughts:

Lead with love without a word being said (voice, body language). Set the tone and gather yourself before the meeting. Your nutritionally challenged loved one needs to know you are coming from a good place. Let your spirit dictate the mood and environment. Say a prayer before the meeting if you desire.

Act like this is the only chance you may have to impact your loved one. This is the fourth quarter and the ninth inning. It is important to encompass all your concerns; this is the golden opportunity. Exude confidence and your loved one will see you put effort into this conversation. Use your list as a double check. Do not read it like a robot. If need be, write your concerns in a letter and read the letter if you feel nervous and think you may forget things.

Show true love and compassion toward your loved one. Pick your words wisely and have a caring tone. Tell your loved one that you want them to be around for a long time. Touch is important; let them know you care. Look your loved one in the eyes. Nonverbal communication is more important than ever. The fear of the unknown is prevalent at this stage in the conversation.

Establish an eco-system designed to help your loved one thrive. It is good to have family members buy-in to execute the plan that is established. Ask your loved what would help them accomplish goals. Let your loved one lead this discussion.

Let them think about everything that was said and give them space. What you are sharing is hard to hear. Don't be resentful if they get angry. Keep your heart open without having your love become closed. Remember, you can't change someone. As the supporter, don't forget to take care of yourself. If you are not healthy in your mind, body, and spirit, you cannot help others.

-10-

THE TIPPING POINT

We went to South Africa for the first time in 1997, a few years after apartheid had officially ended there. Butch was invited to be the keynote speaker at a global medical conference of surgeons and gynecologists that was held in Sun City Resort, about two hours outside of Johannesburg. As we took the long car ride from Johannesburg to Sun City, I marveled at the fact that this modern Africa wasn't the one I had envisioned from seeing films, documentaries, and reading books.

At Sun City Resort and Casino, we were treated like royalty by the hotel staff. It was clear they were privy to our arrival. As soon as Butch stepped out of the car, all eyes were on him. Butch's 6'4" 450-pound frame demanded respect. The onlookers were startled by this massive man, but soon it was obvious the pride of such a prestigious black man entering their hotel, especially on the heels of apartheid, seemed to overshadow his physical appearance.

After checking in and being waited on hand and foot by the staff, we settled in our suite. It was so nice to be away, yet I was far away from my precious one-year-old twin girls. I remember feeling guilty because we were going to miss their birthday. They would turn one without Mommy and Daddy there. Even though I knew they wouldn't remember us not being there, it still bothered me. I missed them desperately, but getting away together was what we both needed. Being the mother of five (including a set of twins) and being married to a surgeon can be at times more than one can handle. I needed a break!

After the long flight to Africa, all I wanted to do was go to sleep. Unfortunately, wanting to settle in for the evening was not an option for us. We were invited to an opening dinner ceremony for the conference, so we had to get freshened up, changed, and go quickly downstairs. Getting Butch anywhere on time is a miracle within itself. He was always chronically late. In an effort to move this process along, I told Butch to go in the bathroom first because as always, I can get changed and cleaned up in record time, especially for a girl. While waiting for Butch to get done, I took a breather and rested my body. As I lay peacefully across the bed, I marveled at how blessed I was to be in Africa. Africa was always on my "bucket list," but I never dreamed it would happen. I couldn't wait to get settled in, sign up for a safari, and see all the sights I had fantasies about. I loved the "Wild Kingdom" television show as a child and so being out in the "bush" was more than a dream come true for me.

Crisis!

As I started to drift off to sleep to take a much-needed catnap while Butch got ready, I heard a loud crash and scream come from the bathroom. At first, I thought I might be dreaming, but when I heard my name called frantically, I knew this was no dream. Was this the incident that I had always envisioned— Butch having a heart attack? The anxiety that I carried with me due to his weight challenge haunted me at every turn. The "what ifs" were my constant companions.

> *I found myself constantly worried about the "what ifs."*
> *What if he had a heart attack?*
> *What if a fall crippled him?*
> *What if he fell asleep while driving?*
> *I had no escape from the "what ifs."*

I hated being a slave to the "what ifs," but did not know how to shake them. Day and night they haunted me. Even while in another country on a once-in-a-lifetime trip, they showed up again. I think somehow I looked to escape the world of obesity for a bit. My trip to Africa was a fantasy escape from the day-to-day anxieties I faced back home. I dreamed of a different reality, even if it was just for a week. New people, scenery, and open mindedness about those who are obese, that's what I hoped for in Africa.

As my name was called yet again, I couldn't for the life of me envision what could have happened behind that bathroom door.

I yelled, "Butch, are you okay?"

My thoughts raced as I ran to a scene that I will never forget. Nothing could have prepared me for what I saw next. My husband had sat on the commode and broke it into pieces. Water and debris were everywhere. I remember him looking up at me with this pitiful look as to say, "Please help me." The look in his eyes was so much more than, "Help me out of this situation."

I saw on his face the pained plea...

"Help me with my challenge—morbid obesity!"

I was paralyzed.

I couldn't speak.

A myriad of mixed and contradictory feelings overwhelmed me.

Like popcorn, questions came immediately to the tip of my tongue:

Are you okay?
How do you feel?
Can you get up?
Should I call someone for help?
Are you hurt?
What are we going to do?
What happened?

Yes, believe it or not, I wanted to ask, "What happened?" However, that was a dumb question. The situation was self-explanatory. *His obesity had shattered the toilet.*

I could feel the shame, embarrassment, and fear as if an IV was connected from his soul to mine. If he hurt, I hurt, and the hurt was unbearable. However, I could not show it outwardly because he looked to me for strength, and I (his wife, enabler, rescuer, fixer, and protector) would not let him down.

What a minute! Hit the pause on the replay video of this moment. My friend reading this book, let's get up close and personal. If this had been your loved one, what would you have asked, felt, thought, and done? John F. Kennedy is often quoted as having said the Chinese word for "crisis" contains two characters meaning "danger" and "opportunity." While his Chinese interpreting was incorrect,[3] his understanding of a crisis from my perspective was right on for the situation facing Butch and me. You can worry about, deny, ignore, or rationalize your loved one's "nutritional challenge," but the truth is, one day you must face it, not fantasize about escaping it. Morbid obesity is both a chronic crisis and a dangerous emotional and health crisis about to happen. You can choose now to take the *opportunity* that reading this book has afforded you to be **proactive** or be **reactive** to the *danger* that will befall you both!

What did I do? In true "Dana form," I immediately got him up and helped clean up everything before we both made the hard trip downstairs to tell those people so proud that my husband had graced their hotel, what had happened.

My dream fantasy had turned into a nightmare. Honestly, I wanted to die. My insides screamed with embarrassment, fear, anxiety, frustration, and most of all, guilt, for feeling all the above. I wanted to help this sweet man with his weight challenges so badly, but I didn't know how. He looked to me for strength through this catastrophe, and I was determined not to let him down no matter how I felt. I wanted him to be able to count on me (*enable him*) through thick and thin.

Our Crisis Became My "Tipping Point"

Leave it to mother Africa to imprint such a life-changing experience for the both of us. Looking back, it was such a paradox for Butch. On the one hand, it was one of the proudest moments I believe in Butch's career to be an African American keynote speaker on the heels of apartheid, and yet at the same time experiencing one of the lowest moments of his life. For me, this was my "tipping point."

Malcolm Gladwell, author of *The Tipping Point,* defines a "tipping point "as the moment of critical mass, the threshold, or the boiling point. This was my moment of critical mass. I could no longer force my weary spirit to an infinity of "it's okays" when I knew good and well it was not okay. The love I had for Butch never wavered, but I knew I would have to take care of myself enough to own my authentic feelings about his weight.

My "tipping point" was when his health challenges forced me to the realization that I had to help myself before I could help him.

I subsequently started going to counseling, working out again, taking art classes, and rekindling some friendships. I rediscovered "who Dana was," and to my surprise, my husband took notice and asked if he could workout with me. What a turnaround!

We realized we are not meant to be perfect, but we are meant to be whole. Actually, the Greek word *telos* (often translated "perfect") means "to be complete, whole, reach the end, and finished." Let me ask you, "What is your end game?"

I'm saying to you right now that I understand, and I get what you're going through because I've lived it. Those of you who are silently suffering with the challenge of living and loving someone who is obese/morbidly obese/nutritionally challenged do not have to shrink back or hide anymore. I understand and want to help, support, motivate, and empower you to take care of yourself while continuing to support your loved ones.

Sometimes you will never know the value of a moment until it becomes a memory.
-Dr. Seuss

Ask yourself...

- *Where are you headed with the crisis of your loved one's nutritional challenges?*
- *Are you and your relationship a train wreck waiting to happen, a dangerous crisis about to tip toward a huge crash—emotionally and physically?*

- *Is this moment, right now, are you going to take this opportunity to help yourself and become proactive?*
- *Or, will you slip back into denial, fantasyland, and sleepless nights worrying about your "what ifs"?*

Would You Take These Actions?

- Make a list of what you need to do to start helping yourself. List one or more persons who you can ask to support you.
- Put dates on the list of when you will start each self-help action on your list.
- Share your list with your loved one or friend who will hold you accountable to "just do it."
- Write a simple prayer asking God to grant you courage, determination, power, and the endurance to envision your *telos*—your finish line for becoming whole and complete.

-11-

THE DECISION

---

*D*id he just say gastric bypass surgery? I know Butch needs and wants to lose weight, but there has to be another way. What about new and improved diet pills, a diet that we haven't heard of, or what about anything other than surgery? Unbeknownst to me, Butch had been contemplating this decision for a long time. A previous patient of his had called him from her hospital bed while recovering from the gastric bypass surgery.

Butch had removed her gallbladder in the Dominican Republic about a year prior to her calling him. At that time, she weighed close to 350 pounds (i.e. morbidly obese). She recognized what a gifted surgeon he was. The cruel reality was the challenge they both faced (obesity) could compromise their dreams of a long life. She decided to have the gastric bypass surgery by a fellow colleague of Butch's, Dr. Phil Schauer, who at the time was at the University of Pittsburgh Medical Center (UPMC). Ironically, Butch had trained Dr. Schauer in a laparoscopic skills course years prior when Butch was a professor at Yale. As she laid recovering from this life-altering surgery, she thought about Butch and the struggle they shared. She thought about all the lives he could continue to save, but feared if he didn't do something drastic, the world would lose a gift. She felt it was time for Doctor Butch to take steps and heal himself.

So, she called Butch and told him about her decision to have the surgery. She shared with him how she thought it would be a good option for him as well. Usually, Butch would have become defensive or angry if someone other than me would bring up a concern about his weight. However, he didn't react negatively because he knew she was came from a good place and only wanted the best for him. She wanted him to stay alive, as we all did.

My Issues About His Surgery

Honestly, I had mixed emotions about the surgery. I didn't know the ins and outs of gastric bypass surgery. I had heard of stomach stapling, but I wasn't even sure if that was the same procedure. **Gastric bypass surgery** refers to a surgical procedure in which the stomach is divided into a small upper pouch and a much larger lower remnant pouch and then the small intestine is rearranged to connect to both.[4] My emotions about this possible option were all over the place. On one hand, I was relieved this could be the blessing we hoped for to finally assist Butch with his weight loss. On the other hand, I thought we had not yet done the due diligence necessary to come up with another solution.

I had often blamed myself for Butch's nutritional challenges. Could I have prepared healthier meals? Maybe I should have encouraged him to exercise more, or I could have surfed the net more aggressively to find out new improved diet plans, pills, weight loss centers, etc. I felt like this surgery could give our family the quality of life that we deserved, but at what cost? What if he died during the surgery? How could I go on? How could I raise our children alone? What if the surgery didn't work? What if, what if, and so on?

What if **can become an excuse, denial, or fearful avoidance of the reality and dangers of morbid obesity.**

I often thought people would think I made him do it or I suggested he take this drastic step. All these thoughts inundated my being constantly; the "demonic thoughts committee" in my head met 24/7.

For some reason, I couldn't let myself go to a place of optimism about this surgery. Don't ask me why—it was hard. I knew this would be an insurmountable hurdle that we as a family unit would have to climb. Maybe I wanted to stay neutral for him in case the procedure didn't work. I had no reference point on how to react to this situation. I always worked so hard to make him comfortable by diverting the outcome of his challenges, and this one was no different. Honestly, it was exhausting. I wanted to stay positive, but cautious, supportive yet true to my feelings. It was a balancing act to say the least and one that Butch had no idea I struggled with daily.

Of course, I daydreamed about how different our lives could be with Butch at a normal weight; the big differences it would make and the little ones. For example, the constant worrying about his health would subside. We could finally sit together side by side at the movie theatre like other couples I envied. Butch could be mobile enough to enjoy playing with the kids in the backyard or be able to sit on the rides with them at the amusement parks. Oh how I prayed the constant judgments that he had to endure daily from strangers and his colleagues would subside. Yes, this would be a dream for our entire family—one that I could only hope might come true.

Butch, on the other hand, was sure about this option. Being a physician, he knew all the ins and outs of this procedure, but what I didn't know was he had been secretly contemplating it even before his former patient had approached him. I was a bit surprised, because I never recalled him bringing this up. I remember we had talked about exploring different options, but never one this serious.

Butch had made up his mind. He wasn't asking me if he should do it. Rather, he simply and candidly informed me. He wasn't arrogant in his stance, but matter of fact about it. He told me that he loved his life with the kids and me and he wanted to be alive for all the many millions of memories we would continue to make together. He felt like this was his last resort. The sincerity I felt in his heart was one that would not let me be anything but supportive. I heard him. He loved me so much that he was willing to risk his life to save his life. How do you not support that?

Acting on the Decision

The next thing I knew, Butch had called Dr. Schauer and asked him if he would do his surgery. Of course, he graciously agreed. As Butch prepared for the surgery over the next few months, my feelings and thoughts became a blur to me. The process of getting approval from the insurance company brutal, but Butch never wavered in his desire to make this surgery become a reality. The surgery would take place out of town in Pittsburgh where Dr. Schauer practiced, which made this even more challenging. The countless doctor appointments, phone calls, evaluations, and paperwork did not shake Butch's resolve. His mind was made up; this surgery would happen. It was the beginning of a new chapter for team Rosser. Was I up for the challenge?

Butch and Dana on a boat

Ask Yourself...

- *Have you both explored all options for moving forward toward overcoming your nutritional challenges including surgery if it is a viable option?*
- *What fears do each of you have regarding each option?*
- *What possibilities and hopes does each option present?*
- *Will others' opinions (good or bad) sway your decision to move forward?*

Would You Take These Actions?

- Are you willing to sit down with your loved one and make a priority list of all your options while openly sharing your fears and hopes?

- If not, why not? If so, when will you do it and will you plan enough time and space to privately discuss and plan without the interruptions of children, work, phone, or other distractions? In making this plan, who is assigned to researching the facts about each option?
- If gastric bypass is an option, would you consider attending a bariatric support group meeting to learn more about the process?
- Would you be willing to attend an Overeater's Anonymous meeting to learn every aspect of this disease?

-12-

THE SURGERY

As my husband Butch lay flat on his back on a hospital gurney about to be wheeled out of the room for gastric bypass surgery, I reminisced about all the fun-filled times we had shared together. His contagious Cheshire cat smile that captured me the first time we met had reverted into a peaceful humbled grin that somehow whispered gently to me, "Dana, this is the right thing to do." God willing, if the surgery succeeded, we would have a fresh start in life, but the realization that he could die in surgery was more than I could bear.

He looked up at me and said, "Dana, I love you, and I'm doing this for us. I need you to be strong. Please just pray for me."

I nodded and whispered, "I love you, too."

I released his soft, tender hand. As the attendants wheeled him away, and the double doors swung shut behind him, I stood in disbelief. My personal interrogation started:

- *How did we get here?*
- *Is there something more I could have done to prevent this operation?*
- How could you let him do this, Dana? *I beat myself up relentlessly.*

The fear, guilt, and worry ate away at my fragile soul. For the next three hours, I sat in the waiting room inconsolable and seemingly involuntarily holding my breath. As I cried a river of tears, I thought about our journey together and my deep love for him. I knew this was the right thing to do; it didn't "feel" good, if that makes sense. I was physically tired and emotionally spent.

Several days before the surgery, Butch and I flew to Pittsburgh to get settled into our hotel and to take care of any last-minute appointments before surgery. If worrying about Butch wasn't enough, I had to leave behind our four-year-old twin babies for close to two weeks. The amount of stress on me was crippling. I had never been away from my babies that long. I remember trying to explain to the twins that Mommy and Daddy had to go away for a little while because Daddy needed an operation. At that age, they could only understand a little of what was going on. All they were worried about was when we would come back. To them, their Daddy was a big playful teddy bear. They were too young to know the real danger of his condition.

On the contrary, it was hard when we told the older kids (Kevin, Duane, and Nikki). I remember them looking concerned. Nikki broke down and cried. They had always spoken to me about their concern for their dad's health. So, in a way, I think they were relieved about the prospects of the weight loss, but also scared of the risk.

Talking to Butch about his weight in a family setting was sort of taboo. It was the pink elephant in the room. We would always talk about his weight behind his back. When we brought up the surgery at dinner, it was awkward to be speaking of it so openly. In spite of their initial reservations, they were super supportive. I will say, though, other family members were not as supportive. They talked more about the risks of the surgery rather than the benefits. It's funny because these same family members were the main ones criticizing him for being morbidly obese. In a sense, he couldn't win in their eyes. That was sad to me. Butch had to go into this surgery knowing he didn't have everyone's blessing. I do understand at the root of all this was fear of the unknown, but on the other hand, if he did nothing, death would have been inevitable. It was just a matter of time.

Preparing for the Big Day

There were so many things that I needed to prepare before Butch's big day. I had to make sure I had all the approved foods on the list that were given to me for post op bariatric patients. Broths, non-sugar drinks, Jell-O, water, etc., would be Butch's diet after surgery for a while until he progressed to pureed foods. This was all so new for me. Butch would eat broth and pureed foods, *for real*?

After his surgery, I was told he would eat much smaller portions. I couldn't even imagine that. I often wondered if I would be able to eat in front of him without him feeling deprived or feeling guilty for eating regular food. The last thing I wanted to do was to entice him to backslide into his old habits. I must admit I was a bit selfish in that I didn't want to eat broths, Jell-O, etc., because he had to. Lord knows I loved him, but I would not have been able to sustain that diet—*no way*!

Butch's comfort after the surgery was another big component. It was recommended I purchase body pillows for Butch. A lot of times, right after surgery, some bariatric patients can't lie down in the bed to sleep because of the pain. It's more comfortable for them to be upright when they sleep—hence the pillows. All the instructions from Dr. Schauer's support staff were helpful, but also intimidating to say the least. Because I'm such a perfectionist, I had to have everything on that list precise and to a "t." I realized this was not an operation for Butch, but we embarked on a "lifestyle change" for our whole family. I would gladly do all this again and again if it meant I would have my "Butchie baby" with me longer on this earth.

Butch, the God-gifted surgeon, was helpless under the knife and I prayed for one more chance to tell him that I loved him no matter what. I would do anything to keep him with me. My prayer was a mantra I said over and over again: ***Please God, just let him live.*** After about three hours, I finally saw his surgeon, Dr. Schauer, come into the waiting room.

He said, "Dana, Butch is okay; he did fine."

Those words were music to my ears. Thank God; my husband was okay.

I immediately asked if I could see him, and he said, "Of course."

As I walked down the long hall to see him, I felt so grateful to be alive and witness the new birth of my husband. When I finally got to see him, I kissed him and said:

> *"I'm so proud of you.*
> *I love you.*
> *You made it.*
> *God was smiling on you.*
> *We're going to make the best of this, and I'm here for you.*
> *Whatever you need, I've got your back."*

Butch in hospital after surgery   Butch and Dr. Phil Schauer

Ask yourself...

- *When you and your loved one finally do choose an option that's best for both of you, will you write down and then follow through on preparing to do it?*
- *Remember, your plan cannot be a "let's try it and see what happens." Your preparations must be for success and moving forward, regardless of any temporary setbacks. What feelings, thoughts, and positive actions are you embracing as you move forward?*
- *Is this the best decision for the family? Keep them in the loop.*

Would You Take These Actions?

- Write down your preparation plans for the decision you both have made. Sign and date it.
- As you implement your plan, keep a journal that you both can share with each other to help encourage one another.
- Would you be willing to implement plan B if plan A doesn't work?

-13-

THE TRANSFORMATION

Facing Changes after Surgery or Significant Weight Loss

As with most major surgeries, the patient will be weak and groggy for the first couple of days. I must say, unlike most doctors, Butch was a model patient. He was up and walking several hours after his surgery. I was so proud of him. Fortunately, Butch had no complications and was discharged from the hospital three days after surgery. Because he had his surgery in Pennsylvania (our home was in Connecticut), we stayed at a nearby hotel until he went back for his post-op check-up. Dr. Schauer wanted to see Butch within seven to ten days after surgery.

> **When your loved one's eating habits and choices change, your family may experience culinary chaos for a while.**

Eating Changes. Unfortunately, I was not prepared for the culinary chaos that Butch experienced once we did get back home. He would tell me he wanted to try a certain dish and I would gleefully make it for him. Then he would change his mind and want something different. After about seven changes, he got on my nerves. The one thing that I learned was Butch went through a taste-bud brouhaha. Nothing tasted the same, which caused culinary chaos. I am not sure medically what was happening, but what I observed was somehow, the tongue, stomach, and mind had one big misunderstanding. I had to fight hard to not take it personally.

Even though I am a great cook and it took little effort for me to warm up some soup, I felt discombobulated with all those "demands." Looking back now, I was truly scared. Butch wasn't demanding these things from me. It was my own insecurity in feeling that I would not be able to pacify him after his surgery. I think his indecisiveness took Butch by surprise as well. I think the pain of the surgery, the instant change of his appetite, and the lack of food satisfying him as it did before caused him to have the blues. I thought to myself, *What did this surgery do to him?*

Mood changes. The other major change that I noticed in Butch was the moodiness. Because of the culinary chaos, food was no longer his "lover." Food had given Butch great joy and comfort. Now, that had changed. I equate it to someone going through rehab for a drug addiction. He literally went through somewhat of a "withdrawal." He wanted to eat a specific food, but couldn't, so he became moody. He no longer had food as an escape for any pain he tried to smooth over. He tried to recalibrate his life right before my eyes. It was bittersweet to say the least.

This was a difficult time for me as well and I would advise loved ones to communicate their honest feelings with each other during this period. Having a physician, pastor, psychologist, bariatric support groups, counselor or even a trusted friend to talk to for support is important, and something I wish I had done.

As Butch progressed in his recovery, we would venture out to eat at local restaurants. I was always a bit apprehensive about it because there were so many variables. What if we got there and he couldn't find anything he liked on the menu? What if he ate something that didn't agree with him and he immediately got sick? What if he ordered something, didn't like it, and then got moody? I remember always feeling a bit awkward when ordering something Butch could not have. At this point in the process, he could only have soft foods. I could tell he was bummed out about it. He would often want us to order one entrée (soft foods) and split it because honestly, he would barely eat anything. I didn't mind, but I didn't want to have to be tied down to a meal he craved or could tolerate. Sometimes, I wanted the dish I liked and I didn't want to always share. I had to draw the line somewhere. I felt I had sacrificed a lot and I wanted what I wanted. You could call me selfish and you're probably right, but you could also call me human.

The other thing was we could never agree on which dish to get when we decided to share. I felt like I was forced to have to change my likes and dislikes because of his dietary restrictions. Yes, I became resentful. Yes, I still wanted to help and support him, however, his eating lifestyle drastically changed, not mine. Nonetheless, we went through the changes together. It was new territory for both of us. No one sat down with me to tell me about all the changes that would directly affect and involve me. Here's the good news for you: I am telling you in advance, so prepare yourself for mood swings that both of you will have.

Be Proactive!

After several weeks, Butch's appetite began to stabilize, and I began to figure him out. It was so weird seeing him eat less than my four-year-old twins. He also could not eat some of the foods that he had enjoyed before. Breyer's ice cream, milk-based products, and anything high in sugar were not Butch's friends anymore. He developed some lactose intolerance.

Butch, Dana, and the twins at their first grade formal (Snow Ball-2003).

Another thing I had to modify was how much I cooked. I have never been one to cook a little bit of anything. After all, you never know who would stop by and want something to eat. At the time, it was just the four of us at home, and because of Butch's new diet, we initially wasted a lot of food. I had to gradually learn how to cut back on the amount of food I cooked. Also, I noticed my personal serving sizes were much bigger than Butch's plate and that disturbed me. Lord knows I did not want him to get thinner while I got bigger. I learned along with Butch to be more mindful of when I was full, hence, I didn't eat as much as I had before.

Moving into a New Lifestyle for Both of Us

Because of Butch's new lifestyle, I tried to make meals even healthier. For me, this was not a big change, because I tried to do a lot more baking and broiling instead of frying, and eating more fish and chicken than pork and red meat even before the surgery. So, I stepped up my game and included even more vegetables and fruits.

If I did have "junk food" in the house, I would have baked potato chips, and low-fat yogurt/ice cream, etc. I figured we all needed to start eating healthier to help "Big Daddy" sustain his weight. I made it a family affair. However, I must say, at times, Butch could become like a reformed smoker and point out things that I should not eat or the kids should not eat. I truly understand he was trying to help, but he had to let me "sin a little." He felt because he couldn't have it, then nobody should have it. I had to have my chocolate every now and then. He would become an expert about how many fat grams were in something and then give a lecture series on the subject. So many times I wanted to say, "Listen, you had the surgery, not me, so lay off."

The truth is, we made many lifestyle changes regarding nutrition, fitness, communication, attitudes toward food, and understanding one another through positive, affirming sharing of feelings, thoughts, and changing behaviors. Prepare yourself for positive change! Remember, you are "for" each other without trying to "control" or "parent" one another.

Nikki's wedding

The Transformation

To see Butch lose so much weight so fast was amazing. To see him try on his clothes and say, "Hey Dana, look how big my clothes are getting," was the best feeling in the world for both of us. Knowing that because of this operation, his quality of life would be so much better and give our family a chance of enjoying life to the fullest, was a blessing. His transformation happened right before my eyes. Little things like being able to tie his own shoes, snoring less, becoming more agile, or easily fit into his car without having to do a *Cirque du Soleil* routine were some of the many things that shifted.

Before the surgery, he suffered with sleep apnea. With the weight loss and the help of a c-pap machine, his sleep apnea was no longer an issue. He got a good night's sleep and was more alert and energetic. One of the most memorable moments by far for me was when we returned to Disneyland several years after the surgery and he was able to ride on the Space Mountain roller coaster for the first time. As he gingerly pulled the safety bar down, anticipating the worse, it locked into place and I remember he burst into tears. He could barely catch his breath. You could tell at that moment there was a sense of "normalcy" that overtook him. I honestly think he was surprised the bar was able to lock in place. He wept like a baby and so did I. We cried and laughed through the whole ride. What a full-circle moment. It's funny, because even after he lost a ton of weight, Butch told me that when he would look in the mirror, he would still see himself as 460 pounds. It took a while for his mind and eyes to catch up with his physical reality. It amazed me how he couldn't see what I saw; he was always so critical of himself.

Everyone is so proud of their nutritionally challenged loved one after the weight loss, and they soaked up all the attention and rightfully so. So, why are feelings of insecurity, jealousy, and fear starting to creep up within you? Honestly, I never had feelings of jealousy, but I must admit I was insecure and fearful. Why? You may ask. As I had mentioned earlier, I have deep rooted abandonment issues and anytime anything bumps into that hurt, I cringe. So, I always thought Butch would leave me one way or another. Either by a heart attack (pre-op) or leave me for someone else because he thought he was now Denzel Washington (post-op). Crazy, I know.

Remember, the spouse is the person with the most at stake for change in the bariatric patient's life. They love their mate, however, they are also "losing" some version of them. Spouses can react in many different ways, but for the most part, they will adjust favorably. I want to encourage you to read *Relationship Challenge Before and After Weight Loss Surgery* by Walter Medlin M.D. FACS.[5]

Sadly, the divorce rate for bariatric patients is high. In researching this subject, there are many websites that describe weight loss surgery and list divorce as one of the possible post-op complications. One site goes as far as to call it "bariatric divorce." After bariatric surgery, the rules of marriage can often change. One person in a marriage gets the surgery. They lose weight. They start looking good. The other one either gets jealous or doesn't want to be married to them anymore. This is so tragic, but true.

I know not everyone may go through these feelings, but so many supporters I have talked to about this have had similar feelings. I will never forget the first time I saw a woman blatantly checking Butch out. I was appalled, shocked, scared, flattered, and mad. I had never experienced other women checking him out before in that manner. I always felt he was a handsome guy despite his weight challenge, but I was so used to seeing people stare at Butch in disdain and with critical looks that it was foreign to me to see looks of admiration. It took me some time to process this new situation.

How others look at your spouse may change. Get ready for new perceptions by others toward both of you.

I was scared because I thought, *Oh my God, other women are checking him out, and they are going to make a move on him. He is going to leave me.* It did not dawn on me that Butch had a responsibility in that equation. I was irrational, I know. My husband never gave me any reason to think he would cheat on me, but my mind took that fantasy and ran with it. I had him divorced from me and married to some other hot-looking woman.

I began a whole regime of irrational thinking. *I had better hit the gym some more and get in shape or he will definitely get rid of me. Why would he do that? What if he did do that? I would be so angry. After all, I had been with him through thick and thin, and now he thought he was all that and going to leave me? I think not!* I was delusional, but I'm telling you, these feelings are all *too real* for those supporting obese loved ones.

Even though I did not experience real jealousy, I know a lot of supporters who have. After all, some of the supporters I know have received all the attention while their challenged spouses have been invisible to others. Then, having to share the limelight is a big adjustment. You may think that sounds silly, selfish, and childish to feel that way, but that's a reality for some, believe me. *Feelings are real, even if they are not reality.* Whether they are reality or not, own your feelings. One of the reasons I wrote this book was to express feelings that may not sound popular.

Butch and Dana toasting at Jack and Jill event (Texas, 2009)

Ask Yourself…

- *If weight loss surgery is an option for your loved one, will you be ready for the changes you may encounter?*
- *Are you prepared for the attention your loved one may receive after a significant weight loss?*
- *Do you have any fears that once your loved one has lost the weight, they will gain it back?*

Would You Consider Taking These Actions?

- Attend a support group for spouses/loved ones to learn more about the effects of bariatric surgery post-op.
- Alter your eating habits while in the company of your loved one.
- Exercise together to stay fit.

-14-

"I Didn't Know That!"

Dana's candid conversation with her hubby Dr. James "Butch" Rosser...

Butch and Dr. Oz

"In what ways did you feel your obesity affected me, if at all?" I asked Butch one day.

Butch thought about it for a minute and then said, "From a pure reflex standpoint, I think I felt you would eventually wake up from this mysterious dream that you had found yourself engulfed in, and say, 'This is crazy as hell. Let me out of here now.' Eventually, I felt it would be something that would drive you away."

Somewhat surprised by his response, I asked, "So, you didn't feel like I loved you enough to work through it with you? What did you think I suffered from?"

"From my standpoint," Butch said candidly, "I felt no human being short of God Almighty would have enough love to help a spouse overcome the weight of being nutritionally challenged. Eventually, I thought it would be too much for a person like you to overcome, even though you had all the best aspects of nurturing in your heart. So, I have lived in fear that I'd wake up one day and you'd be gone."

"Wow! I didn't realize you thought one day, I would leave," I mused. "Well, if that is the case, I don't understand why you married me then."

"It was like I was riding a wave and this tsunami of joy suddenly came rolling in. I stayed on the surfboard to ride it as long as I could. You touched my life, and no matter what the longevity was, I would be better off than not experiencing it at all. It's similar to the way I have lived my whole life. I figured one day, I would not wake up. I would die in my sleep. One day, the burden of being with me would be too much for you to overcome and you would leave."

"But you saw I married you in spite of that, so why would you still think I would leave?" I asked. "Didn't you believe I loved you?"

"I thought I was the recipient of an unbelievable dream," Butch explained, "and God had given you to me. I actually looked at you as extending your hand in love to me, but I did not bring any assets to the party or to you. It was like our life together was like this ledger and you were on the negative end of a ledger, and eventually the whole thing would go bankrupt."

Feeling he was open and honest with me, I decided to ask the big question, "Did that make you want to lose weight?"

"Well, to be honest with you, I wanted to," he answered sadly, "but all my attempts had not been successful. So, I wondered if I would ever achieve that goal."

Did You Feel Loved?

Hurting for him, I asked, "Did I make you feel unlovable, or unwanted?"

"No," he answered quickly. "Just the opposite. You made me feel unbelievably loved and unbelievably wanted. I mean, you should be a Medal of Honor recipient if this was a war. You have gone above and beyond the call of duty to show me what true love and commitment could be. I always felt bad things would happen to me because of my inability to overcome this problem. In a way, it's kind of sick, but I thought if I couldn't get everything together, I didn't deserve it."

"Well, I know you considered surgery as a way to handle this challenge, but I am curious as to how you felt our relationship might change once you had the surgery?"

"I don't know if I thought about change because our relationship was so solid to begin with, but I guess in a way I thought the dark cloud that was over my head would be removed," Butch answered with a smile. "I definitely thought everything would get even better."

"Name one specific thing that you thought was going to get better," I asked, wondering what he would to say.

"Well, to be honest with you, the comfort level of being out in public with me," he answered. "I hoped you could become less of a target of inquisition. You know what I'm saying because I knew that was going on."

"Really?" I asked totally surprised. "You never told me that."

"No matter who we are, how successful we become, every individual sees our outward appearance first. So, from a logical point of view, it would stand to reason that the first thing most people would see would not be my heart or my struggle. They see the physical presentation of you and me together," he explained, "I know that challenges the boundaries of rationale for most people. I know they ask themselves why you are with me."

"What about your kids?" I asked, realizing he knew about all those times I tried to protect him from the ridicule of others. "How do you think your obesity affected your children?"

"Well, I worried about them being ashamed and about them being ridiculed," Butch said, but then he smiled and added, "They did a beautiful job of never bringing it up. They always expressed how proud they were of my success as a surgeon."

"Did you always feel helpless about your condition, like there was no help for you?" I asked him. "Did you ever feel this was your lot in life? I know from what you have told me before that you tried a lot of different ways to lose weight before considering the surgery."

"Well, early on, I had what I call a "Michael Jordan mantra." That is when you know the game is on the line, but you have this delayed sense of urgency until suddenly you are in the fourth quarter and you know you need to do something or you are going to lose," he patiently explained. "For me, there were certain physical events that were turning points and pushed me into that fourth quarter urgency."

Turning Points

"Turning points? Like what?" I asked, realizing there was a lot I did not know about this man I loved.

"One was when I was in a car accident and I had to be cut out of that car. As I sat with the snow falling in my face, for the first time in my life I felt this sense of mortality. Another time I went to speak at the Geisinger Clinic in Pennsylvania, and the hotel was at the bottom of this hill. I had to go up this hill and I had such a shortness of breath, it concerned me."

"I didn't know about either of those! Have there been other turning points in your life like those?" I asked, curious.

"The other thing that was part of a litany of items that kind of got my attention was when I had a bleeding varicosity. As a doctor, I knew the cause and that these were worse because of the increased abdominal pressure from the central obesity. Then the other thing that made me become afraid and made me feel maybe extraordinary measures would be necessary was what I call, 'The day my belly turned black.' I got out of the shower, and I was forced to look in the mirror, which I always tried to avoid. I noticed my belly was dark and I knew that was a sign of hyperinsulinemia. In other words, because of my weight, my body put out tremendous amounts of insulin to try tokeep me from having diabetes. Once that darkness appeared on my belly, I knew it was a secondary effect of all the insulin and my body became more and more resistant to it. In other words, my system was overloaded. That was an unbelievable moment that prepared my heart and mind to accept the fact I needed to seriously diet and exercise to overcome this problem."

"Wow! You never told me any of this! So did you immediately started to change your diet and exercise?" I inquired.

"It was a step in the right direction. Then there was the sleep apnea. I thought it was associated with weight, so at first it was also a motivation. But then I had the mask (c-pap), which took care of it, so it seemed like it was not a motivating factor. However, eventually I discovered it wasn't fixed, because it was indeed connected to the weight. You didn't know any of this because I kept that kind of physical stuff close to the vest."

"Why didn't you feel like you could share some of these things with me, especially with the shortness of breath?" I asked, sadly.

"Well, I think it highlighted another proof that you were with this soon-to-be-invalid husband. Then my biggest fear would happen as you looked at this balance sheet and decided you were not in a winning game and would walk away."

"Well that's so sad to me," I said, feeling the tears behind my eyes. Trying to avoid crying, I decided to change the subject, "What did food give you then that it doesn't give you now since the surgery?"

"Comfort. I think it was comfort," Butch answered after thinking about it for a minute.

"It doesn't bring the same level of comfort now?" I asked.

"No, because I now have so many other things in my life that I allow to give me comfort. I allow my children and you to bring me that comfort I used to get from food. I look forward to time with my family more than anything else. I still like food. I love your cooking, but it does not stand in for the fulfillment I get in living. I went to the water park yesterday, and I was right there with the twins, climbing seven flights of stairs multiple times, and then going down this slide with them, feeling great joy. There's no substance that can replace the kind of joy I get from participating in such activities with my family and making such precious memories."

"Before your surgery, what things would make you happy and give you joy?" I asked, laughing with him as I remembered the fun we had.

"Driving a nice automobile gave me joy, but there were a lot of automobiles I couldn't drive because of my size. I also loved radio-control airplanes. I liked going to the movies, too, but that eventually became an issue because of the seating situation, and then I would often fall asleep and miss most of the movie due to the sleep apnea. It was like a roller coaster. Everything I enjoyed doing was eventually affected by my weight issue."

"So, did you have days when you would wake up in the morning and say, 'Boy, I'm so glad I'm alive'?" I asked.

"No, I generally woke up in the morning with a headache from the sleep apnea. Then the guilt would set in as I realized it was another day I had to face, trying to overcome this issue. I basically beat myself up every morning."

"That's not good," I stated.

"No, that was not good at all. But that's how I felt and that's what I did. So, if you look at it, the strictest definition of the word, there was nothing that gave me pure joy without the downside that was a bummer," Butch said, sadly.

"So, you said you felt God had given me or sent me to you. What was your relationship with God at this time?" I asked, remembering his earlier comment.

"Actually, I thought God had been incredibly generous to me because even though I was in messed-up misery, God gave me you. I was grateful. He brought me back from the depths of absolute destruction, but I did not know whether or not God's plan for me included living a long, productive, happy life. In fact, I hate to say it, but I was sort of at a point where I was resigned to my fate. I never had that sense of total hopelessness, but I was darn close. I existed, day to day in a suboptimal state. I tried working hard, actually over-achieving, because it was like I did not know how much time I had left to make something of my life."

"Even so, it seemed people tended to judge you based strictly on your outward appearance," I commented, thinking how many times I had stared someone down for smirking behind his back. "How did that make you feel?"

"I thought that was absolutely the most antisocial manifestation of the human spirit that you could ever have. I thought people were mean. In fact, I kind of lost hope in the human experience because people were such slum lords as far as their whole outlook toward their fellow human beings was concerned," he shared openly.

Lead with Love

"What could we as a family have done to support you more or could we have done anything differently?" I asked, thinking we could now help others dealing with family issues like this.

"Well, I think what you all did with me was exemplary and something that others could follow. When people behave in a judgmental way, they obviously don't know what's going on. Every second of every day, a person who is nutritionally challenged knows what's going on. Every mirror they pass reminds them of what their life is like. Even when the sun is shining, you see your shadow and are disgusted about the silhouette. If we as a family could have had more organized help such as a counselor to dissect the issues in a fair and balanced way, that would have helped me and the whole family. "

"Really? I had no idea!" I commented honestly. "What can we do to help inform the public about something like this?"

"Yes, and that's the reason it doesn't go away. There's a profound amount of ignorance as to what this is," he said passionately.

I knew I had touched on something important to him. "Isn't it a disease like alcoholism?"

"Frankly, alcoholism and drug abuse have been classified as an illness. That's what legitimized both of them and even helped people seek the cure. But people refuse to embrace the fact that obesity is also a disease. Therefore, most people regard a drug addict with more empathy than an obese person. I think when we're able to overcome this profound amount of ignorance in this country and in the world, then we'll be able to come to grips with helping people who are stricken with this disease. Obese people don't need to be told, 'You're fat.' They need to know where and how to get the right kind of treatment."

What Did Our Family Do Right?

"So, what did we as a family do right, and what did we do wrong in trying to help you overcome and deal with this disease?" I asked.

"Talking about what you all did is a great example. You all led with love. That's not to say you were enablers, but you had appropriate tolerance. Because you led with love and didn't expect "burning bush" moments, I could see you were there for the long haul. You surrounded me with a nurturing type of support. For instance, encouraging walking together as a way to have more time together was an awesome expression of your love and concern for my health. That was a beautiful thing. Changing the way you cooked by decreasing ten to twenty percent of calories was another huge labor of love on your part. It put us both in a healthy attitude, and we were doing it together. All those things were important nurturing components to people like me who are nutritionally challenged. You created a proper support mechanism."

"So, were you surprised to find out all the things I felt when I opened up to you?" I asked, remembering that day we finally faced the reality of our situation together.

"You know, I think you got me to step back and think of that nightmare you experienced. To hear it being said all in one breath like that knocked me flat. The impact was nuclear," Butch said with tears in his eyes. "In fact, it was much worse than what I ever imagined. It was shocking to hear you say it."

"So what do you think had the biggest impact on your final decision to have the surgery?" I asked, wondering how my transparent sharing had added to Butch's decision.

"The number one thing that made me want to step up is I finally got it. I mentioned earlier how people don't classify this as a disease. Well, actually, I didn't either! Here I am, a physician, and I believed all that rhetoric that somehow I was psychologically defective, did not have a strong character, and all those other lies that society projected at people like me all the time. When I actually believed and accepted it was a disease, then I knew what I had to do. There was no other cure for my disease except the surgical route. That's when I became comfortable enough to make an intellectual decision that made me want to take that step. Then, there was those strategically placed emotional components that also helped me move forward with it. The first was your transparent sharing and the second was when one of my patients flew to Santo Domingo in the Dominican Republic to have the surgery. When she shared her plans with me, I had to tell her I suffered with the same problem myself."

"I remember that," I said.

"When she called me from the hospital bed to tell me that she made it through surgery and encouraged me to do the same thing, that was another powerful turning point for me," Butch shared emotionally. "I think that it was a Godsend."

Advice

1. Lead with love.
2. Show them you are there for the long haul.
3. Surround them with a nurturing type of support.
4. Create a proper support mechanism.
5. Lead by example.

Ask Yourself...

- *If you have this kind of conversation with your nutritionally challenged partner, then which of my questions would you ask? Which would you not ask? Why?*
- *If you fear having this conversation with your partner, can you list your fears and share them with a support person?*

Would You Take These Actions?

- Are you ready to have a discussion like this with your partner? If so, what do you need to do to prepare for it?
- Read over the advice I have given you at the end of this chapter. Decide to follow this advice.

-15-

A FINAL WORD OF ENCOURAGEMENT

It has been fourteen years this past August (2015) since Butch had his surgery and life has been good. I wish I could tell you this struggle we both have faced has vanished, but it hasn't. It's a daily battle, but the upside is we are both better equipped now to handle it. Butch has lost about 160 pounds and works hard to keep it off. Has he gained and lost? Yes, but the difference now is that he is aware of when he's full. He's hyper-sensitive if he feels like he's getting off course. He tries to park far away from a store or office in order to walk and get his exercise in. He keeps his doctor appointments and tries to make healthier choices. It's doing the little things that keep him moving forward with controlling his weight.

For me, I have learned I can't control anybody else. I can support and pray for them, but I must leave the rest to God. I love my husband for his courage to want to get better and live. I love him for allowing me to be transparent and share our journey with you all. We will celebrate twenty years of marriage this year. I'm so grateful he is alive and I pray we have many more years ahead of us to love each other *Thru Thick and Thin*. That's where we are, now what about you? What's your next step?

Dana and Butch (June 2015)

Start with a Commitment to Yourself

What makes you happy? Seems like an easy question to answer, but for me it was hard. At one point in my relationship with Butch, I truly strained my brain to come up with something. I think a lot of times when we tend to put others first (especially wives and mothers), we forget who we are. Happiness is such a vague word to me and is often misconstrued. Yes, we can be happy shopping at a mall, picking up a new outfit or eating our favorite meal. However, true happiness is from the inside out and should not be so easily influenced by the world around us.

Ask yourself these questions and seriously consider your answers as I take you through my dealings with my self-discovery:

What is my passion?
Have I prayed about this passion lately?

Is there a cause that I can truly feel strongly about?
What about a hobby that I have put down, that used to bring me such joy?
When is the last time I had coffee with a friend?
Do I ever take a simple walk in the park?

During one of our intimate discussions as we walked through Butch's healing from obesity, I asked him some pointed questions about discovering true happiness and joy. I believe what we learned from each other can help you as well, no matter what you might be battling in your relationships.

"So, do you think that it's helpful that spouses or loved ones speak up about their feelings toward their loved one regarding their weight in a positive way?" I asked as I thought about how transparent I had been about my own feelings with Butch. "Should they share it bothers them and admit it makes them sad or angry? Do you think it would be helpful in moving them forward more aggressively about their weight loss decisions?"

"Well, I think overall happiness is the goal of a relationship, so you have got to bring these feelings to the surface. You can have so much erosion in your relationship that it can no longer stand like a house that is not built on solid ground. You can't let it get to that point. So, I say yes, these things need to come to the forefront, but they need to be brought to the forefront with a sensitivity that is laced with love. The direct confrontational thing is not going to work. You need to get your feelings out, but first there needs to be the little things like what you did before sitting down to the table. For instance, you subtly changed your cooking style and used turkey instead of ham and not having as much sweet stuff in the house. Those are subtle things that didn't help me win the battle, but helped me win the war. If loved ones don't balance their approach of sharing their feelings with helping to provide solutions, it's going to be destructive rather than constructive."

"So, loved ones can lead by example like starting to exercise and take better care of themselves first, then invite their obese family member or loved one to join them and follow suit?" I suggested, catching the constructive concept he conveyed.

"Also, anything that eliminates stress can be a positive way to help a loved one, whether they are dealing with obesity or any other destructive issue. Burying it causes erosion in the relationship, but it should be addressed without adding stress to an already stressful situation," Butch added.

"Can I ask you about when I went through my own bout with depression? Could you tell I was depressed or did you think it was something else?" I asked him.

"Honestly, I think I put it in a bigger, broader category thinking it was the result of the rigors and challenges of being married to me," Butch answered. "The weight was not the only issue. There was a multiplicity of issues that challenged us to have a relationship with balance. The fact of the matter is, at the time I felt like I was under a microscope and what went on around me probably seemed ten times worse than the actual situation. I was basically embedded in unbridled selfishness. Truthfully, I was so caught up in my own pain, I missed a lot of what was going on around me. I think I missed how much you suffered!"

Stop Suffering Silently

Wow! Talk about a reality check! Here I was, trying to help my husband deal with obesity, and all of a sudden, I am dealing with depression. How did this happen? I literally forgot how great life can be. Things that used to bring me so much happiness now seemed out of reach for me as I lost myself in Butch's battle. I literally took on his obesity like I weighed 450 pounds. Now, I am not blaming Butch at all; this was definitely my problem. I had to own this one! I made the decision to take this on; I chose to be morbidly obese without actually carrying the weight. I did not realize I was doing it until one day, it dawned on me that I turned down invitations to go out with my friends, became more and more reclusive, and turned to food for comfort.

This was the life Butch led, and now it bled into my life. I was not being mindful of who I was and what I was supposed to be doing with my life, so I started to pick up Butch's habits and in the process, lost myself. That was when the depression started. I lost my joy and unwittingly traded it in for constant worry. What a terrible trade off that turned out to be, especially when I had no clue I had made that awful decision.

I loved Butch so much, I constantly waited for the other shoe to drop. I lived in fear, praying he wouldn't die of a heart attack. I worried about people ridiculing him at work and felt I needed to be with him to protect him every minute of the day. I wanted to be with my husband for the rest of our lives more than anything else in the world. I truly loved his company, but every time I left him so I could do other things for myself, it left me feeling guilty. I didn't want him to feel bad there were things he couldn't physically do, so I would not do them anymore. Oh, how I desperately wanted him to go to a concert with me or dine out with friends. Even though we sometimes did go out to eat with friends, I knew he did not want to go. Picking up on how uncomfortable he was hurt me, so I wanted to hurry up, finish eating, and get back home to our safe haven where he would not be judged.

Home was the place where I knew Butch was the happiest and where he was safe from the cruel world. Unfortunately, as I cut off social interactions, I didn't realize I cut Dana off from Dana. Learn from my mistakes and please don't stop doing those things that bring you joy and comfort. Butch never wanted me to do that, nor did he ask me to stay with him 24/7. In fact, he never had a clue I went through this inner battle.

Yes, I wanted to tell him what I felt, but I did not want to add to his hurt, so I suffered silently. Constantly protecting him from the bigotry, discrimination, and the out and out cruelty that this disease breeds, I finally learned my arms were too short to box with every problem. It got to the point where I could not let both of us lose this journey we call life—me in some psych ward and my husband in the hospital because of his health challenges. If we did, what would happen to our kids? What example would I set for them? I heard a quote from Dr. Robin Smith: "As parents, we give up the right to self-destruct." How profound!

Not only could I not self-destruct, I couldn't save my man either. I finally realized the cost of giving up who I was would be way too high. How could I be that supporting wife he needed with only half of me functioning? He deserved better than that and so did my family, God, and I did, too.

How many times have you heard the stewardess on a plane say, "In case of an emergency, put on your oxygen mask first before helping others"? I think this principle applies to so many different areas in our lives. As a mother and a wife, it is hard because for the most part, we are born nurturers. We take care of others first and then if we get around to it, we take care of ourselves. It is the nature of the beast. Well, this pattern is not a smart move for anyone, man or woman.

How can I give love, respect, and encouragement to someone when my own tank is not filled with love, respect, and encouragement? How do I effectively take care of anyone else in my family if I'm sitting in a corner somewhere rocking back and forth, singing old nursery rhymes to myself? Oh, I know how to do it; I did it for many years and I paid a high price for it. I lost who I was and I'm sad to say I can never recover that time. However, I feel blessed I can now help others by sharing my mistakes and hopefully shine some light on a delicate situation.

Taking care of yourself goes way beyond getting your hair and nails done. I am talking about making and keeping your own doctor's appointments, having coffee with friends, being spiritually in tune, exercising, and staying healthy. I remember going with Butch to the doctor and sitting in the appointment with him for fear he would not keep the appointment or make an excuse he could not find the office. However, did I show up at the doctor myself when it was time for my physical or would I put it off to another day or whatever lame excuse I could find? Rescheduling was my friend when it came to taking care of me. Do not fall into these same traps. If you truly want to take the best care of your family, no matter what is going on in life, you have to take the best care of yourself first.

Advice

Make new adventures with and without your spouse.

Exercise and take care of you.

Read fun fiction.

Think of creative ways to spend time with your spouse. Make it safe, but fun for both of you.

Don't have unrealistic expectations.

Learn to truly accept them and let them know even if they do not lose one pound, you will still be there.

Never, ever stop laughing.

Find a charity or project where you both can give back in some form or fashion (church, charity group, missions, etc.).

Seek help for both of you. Don't try to do it alone.

Everyone may not need professional help, but seek out help groups like Overeaters Anonymous. Go together as a family project if it is possible and feasible.

Seek out doctors carefully; some doctors can have a terrible bed side manner, which could set you back.

Pray individually and together.

At the beginning of this book, I asked you to read straight through it without pausing at the end-of-chapter questions and suggestion actions. Now I want to encourage you to find a support partner, start a journal, and go through the book one chapter at a time with your support partner as your accountability partner. Answer the questions and journal both your answers and your actions along with how your relationship with your spouse or over-weight partner is progressing. Now the real work begins.

Finally, what I know for sure is that we as supporters have to be whole physically, mentally, and spiritually to be able to handle this challenge and to be an anchor for our loved ones. Personally, I know I couldn't have made it without God's intervention, strength, and love to help me. It may not feel like it or look like it, but never underestimate the power of God in your life. Don't ever forget who is in control. When you can't do anymore, "Stand!" God could be working behind the scenes without you knowing about it. Just know He has got your back!

You can change your mindset, lifestyle, and attitudes. You can support your loved one, but first you must take care of you. I would like to leave you with this prayer by Roy Lessin titled, "Prayer of Release." I pray it will give you hope, strength, and solace throughout your journey. You can do this! Start now.

Prayer of Release

HEAVENLY FATHER, **I release** *to You the burdens that I have been carrying, burdens that You never intended for me to carry.* **I cast** *all my cares upon You—all my worries, all my fears. You have told me to not be anxious about anything, but rather to bring everything to You in prayer with thankfulness.*

FATHER, **calm** *my restless spirit,* **quiet** *my anxious heart,* **still** *my troubling thoughts with the assurance that You are in control. I let go of my grip upon the things I have been hanging onto, with opened hands I come to You.* **I release** *to Your timing all that I am trying to control;* **I release** *to Your timing all that I have been striving to make happen.*

I THANK YOU for Your promise to **sustain** *me,* **preserve** *me, and* **guard** *all that I have entrusted to Your keeping.* **Protect** *my heart and mind with Your peace, the peace that passes all understanding. Father, may Your will be done in my life, in your time, and in Your way.*

Sharing more photos...

Rosser Family Photos (2015)

Resources for You

The following is a list of resources that you and your family can refer to for more information and general support for obesity and weight-related issues. This information is to inform and guide you, but does not replace the opinion or direction of a doctor or professional.

OAC – Obesity Action Coalition

The Obesity Action Coalition (OAC) is the *only* nonprofit organization whose sole focus is representing individuals affected by obesity. Founded in 2005, the OAC remains at the forefront of the fight against obesity. From advocating on Capitol Hill for access to obesity treatments to publishing hundreds of educational resources for individuals affected, the OAC truly represents the voice of all those affected by obesity.

Center for Disease Control & Prevention

The CDC defines obesity and weight issues and offers data and statistics as well as causes and consequences to the disease. You will also find information on programs and additional resources.

American Academy of Pediatrics

Specific information for the prevention and treatment of obesity in children.

Obesity in America

Important news and up-to-date information about obesity and the science and treatment from experts as well as success stories.

Gastric Bypass Surgery

Visit realize.com to learn more about gastric bypass surgery. You will find photos, links and helpful information about what to expect and why it is done and how well it works.

Dana Marie Rosser

Dana M. Rosser is a homemaker, mother, and wife, married to Dr. James "Butch" Rosser Jr., a world-renowned laparoscopic surgeon. Dana is dedicated to educating people on how to support a loved one's challenge with obesity. Dana takes the unique vantage point of offering comfort and understanding from the often overlooked spousal/family members' perspective. Her focus is to lead the mass of supporters out of seclusion, address their emotions, and help them navigate through the delicate issues of caring for a loved one who is "nutritionally challenged." Through her efforts, she hopes to aid in strengthening communication of the family unit as they learn to conquer this obstacle as a unified front.

Dana and Dr. Rosser reside in Orlando, Florida and are the proud parents of five children: Kevin, Duane, Nicole, twins Taylor and Tianna, and two grandchildren, Easton and August.

A native of Akron, Ohio and a graduate of The University of Akron, she enjoys cooking, reading, running, writing, and traveling as a few of her favorite pastimes. Dana has also written articles, is co-author of *Unbreakable Spirit Rising above the Impossible* and has lectured for the National Medical Association (Regional & National), Harvard Patients Safety and Obesity Surgery Conference, and the American Academy of Family Practitioners Conference in regard to this delicate subject.

For more information, resources, and contacting the author go to www. facingobesity.com

ENDNOTES

1 http://www.hsph.harvard.edu/obesity-prevention-source/obesity-consequences/ also, http://www.cdc.gov/obesity/data/adult.html

2 http://www.medscape.com/viewarticle/710209_2

3 http://workplacepsychology.net/2014/08/10/
in-chinese-crisis-does-not-mean-danger-and-opportunity/

4 https://en.wikipedia.org/wiki/Gastric_bypass_surgery

5 http://www.dssurgery.com/images/relationship-challenges-before-and-after-weight-loss-surgery.pdf

CPSIA information can be obtained
at www.ICGtesting.com
Printed in the USA
FFOW02n1559080917
39747FF